REPORT OF THE RIVER MASTER OF THE DELAWARE RIVER

FOR THE PERIOD
DECEMBER 1, 2003–NOVEMBER 30, 2004

Open-File Report 2009–1065

U.S. Department of the Interior
U.S. Geological Survey

CALENDAR FOR REPORT YEAR 2004

DECEMBER 2003

S	M	T	W	T	F	S
	1	2	3	4	5	6
7	8	9	10	11	12	13
14	15	16	17	18	19	20
21	22	23	24	25	26	27
28	29	30	31			

JANUARY 2004

S	M	T	W	T	F	S
				1	2	3
4	5	6	7	8	9	10
11	12	13	14	15	16	17
18	19	20	21	22	23	24
25	26	27	28	29	30	31

FEBRUARY

S	M	T	W	T	F	S
1	2	3	4	5	6	7
8	9	10	11	12	13	14
15	16	17	18	19	20	21
22	23	24	25	26	27	28
29						

MARCH

S	M	T	W	T	F	S
	1	2	3	4	5	6
7	8	9	10	11	12	13
14	15	16	17	18	19	20
21	22	23	24	25	26	27
28	29	30	31			

APRIL

S	M	T	W	T	F	S
				1	2	3
4	5	6	7	8	9	10
11	12	13	14	15	16	17
18	19	20	21	22	23	24
25	26	27	28	29	30	

MAY

S	M	T	W	T	F	S
						1
2	3	4	8	6	7	8
9	10	11	12	13	14	15
16	17	18	19	20	21	22
23	24	25	26	27	28	29
30	31					

JUNE 2004

S	M	T	W	T	F	S
		1	2	3	4	5
6	7	8	9	10	11	12
13	14	15	16	17	18	19
20	21	22	23	24	25	26
27	28	29	30			

JULY

S	M	T	W	T	F	S
				1	2	3
4	5	6	7	8	9	10
11	12	13	14	15	16	17
18	19	20	21	22	23	24
25	26	27	28	29	30	31

AUGUST

S	M	T	W	T	F	S
1	2	3	4	5	6	7
8	9	10	11	12	13	14
15	16	17	18	19	20	21
22	23	24	25	26	27	28
29	30	31				

SEPTEMBER

S	M	T	W	T	F	S
			1	2	3	4
5	6	7	8	9	10	11
12	13	14	15	16	17	18
19	20	21	22	23	24	25
26	27	28	29	30		

OCTOBER

S	M	T	W	T	F	S
					1	2
3	4	5	6	7	8	9
10	11	12	13	14	15	16
17	18	19	20	21	22	23
24	25	26	27	28	29	30
31						

NOVEMBER

S	M	T	W	T	F	S
	1	2	3	4	5	6
7	8	9	10	11	12	13
14	15	16	17	18	19	20
21	22	23	24	25	26	27
28	29	30				

Report of the River Master of the Delaware River for the period December 1, 2003–November 30, 2004

By Bruce E. Krejmas, Gary N. Paulachok, and Stephen F. Blanchard

Open-File Report 2009–1065

U.S. Department of the Interior
U.S. Geological Survey

U.S. Department of the Interior
KEN SALAZAR, Secretary

U.S. Geological Survey
Suzette M. Kimball, Acting Director

U.S. Geological Survey, Reston, Virginia: 2009

For more information about the USGS and its products:
Telephone: 1-888-ASK-USGS
World Wide Web: http://www.usgs.gov/

Suggested citation:
Krejmas, B.E., Paulachok, G.N., and Blanchard, S.F., 2009, Report of the River Master of the Delaware River for the period December 1, 2003–November 30, 2004, U.S. Geological Survey Open-File Report 2009–1065, 82 p.

Contents

Figures

Tables

Conversion Factors and Vertical Datum

Multiply	By	To obtain
Length		
inch (in.)	25.4	millimeter (mm)
foot (ft)	0.3048	meter (m)
mile (mi)	1.609	kilometer (km)
Area		
square mile (mi^2)	2.590	square kilometer (km^2)
Volume		
million gallons (Mgal)	3,785	cubic meter (m^3)
million gallons (Mgal)	1.547	cubic foot per second day (ft^3/s)-d
billion gallons (Bgal)	3.785	cubic hectometer (hm^3)
cubic foot per second day (ft^3/s)-d	0.002447	cubic hectometer (hm^3)
Flow rate		
million gallons per day (Mgal/d)	1.547	cubic foot per second (ft^3/s)
million gallons per day (Mgal/d)	0.04381	cubic meter per second (m^3/s)
billion gallons per day (Bgal/d)	43.81	cubic meter per second (m^3/s)
cubic foot per second (ft^3/s)	0.02832	cubic meter per second (m^3/s)

Datum: Vertical coordinate information is referenced to the North American Vertical Datum of 1988. Horizontal coordinate information is referenced to the North American Datum of 1983.

Temperature in degrees Celsius (°C) may be converted to degrees Fahrenheit (°F) as follows: °F=(1.8x°C)+32

CHEMICAL CONCENTRATIONS

In this report, concentrations of chloride and dissolved oxygen are given in milligrams per liter (mg/L). Milligrams per liter represents the mass of solute (milligrams) per unit volume (liter) of water.

RIVER MASTER LETTER OF TRANSMITTAL AND SPECIAL REPORT

OFFICE OF THE DELAWARE RIVER MASTER
United States Geological Survey
415 National Center
Reston, Virginia 20192

March 17, 2009

The Honorable
John G. Roberts, Jr.
Chief Justice of the United States

The Honorable
Jack A. Markell
Governor of Delaware

The Honorable
Jon S. Corzine
Governor of New Jersey

The Honorable
David A. Paterson
Governor of New York

The Honorable
Edward G. Rendell
Governor of Pennsylvania

The Honorable
Michael R. Bloomberg
Mayor of the City of New York

No. 5, Original.—October Term, 1950
State of New Jersey, Complainant,
v.
State of New York and City of New York, Defendants,
Commonwealth of Pennsylvania and State of Delaware, Intervenors.

Dear Sirs:

For the record and in compliance with the provisions of the Amended Decree of the Supreme Court of the United States entered June 7, 1954, I am transmitting herewith the 51st Annual Report of the River Master of the Delaware River for the 12-month period from December 1, 2003, to November 30, 2004. In this report, this period is referred to as the River Master report year or the report year.

During the 2004 River Master report year, monthly precipitation in the upper Delaware River Basin ranged from 53 percent of the long-term average during February 2004 to 238 percent of the long-term average during September 2004. Total precipitation during the report year was 9.03 inches more than the long-term average. Precipitation during the December to May period, when reservoirs typically refill, was 0.49 inches less than the 63-year average. Precipitation during the report year was below normal in January, February, March, June, October, and November, and above normal in the other six months.

On December 1, 2003, when the report year began, combined storage in the New York City reservoirs in the upper Delaware River Basin was 274.711 billion gallons (Bgal) or 101.4 percent of combined storage capacity. Median combined storage on December 1, computed on the basis of 36 years of record, is 171.931 Bgal. In mid-December, with all reservoirs spilling, the Parties to the Decree established temporary spill reduction programs for Pepacton Reservoir. Storage remained high throughout the year, with spills from at least one reservoir occurring every month. Operations in the basin were conducted as stipulated by the Decree throughout the report year.

On May 6, 2004, the Delaware River Master Advisory Committee met at the Delaware Geological Survey in Newark, Delaware, to discuss hydrologic conditions in the basin and operational procedures for the 2004 reservoir-release season. During the report year, the following individuals served as members of the Advisory Committee:

Delaware	John H. Talley
New Jersey	Samuel A. Wolfe
New York	Sandra Allen
New York City	Michael A. Principe
Pennsylvania	Cathleen Curran Myers

The River Master informed the Advisory Committee that, on the basis of information provided by New York City, the excess-release quantity beginning June 15, 2004, was 8.763 Bgal. Based on reservoir release programs in Delaware River Basin Commission (DRBC) Docket No. D-77-20 CP (Revisions Nos. 7 and 8), the excess-release quantity was to be used for various purposes. On the basis of hydrologic conditions in mid-August, the Parties to the Decree unanimously approved a temporary bottom release program for Cannonsville and Pepacton Reservoirs to reduce the quantity of warm surface-water spills from the reservoirs.

During the report year, the River Master and staff participated in a number of water-supply related meetings of the DRBC. The Deputy Delaware River Master met periodically with representatives of the Parties to the Decree as a member of the Decree Parties Work Group and DRBC's Flow Management Technical Advisory Committee. Issues of particular interest to the River Master involved management of reservoir releases and regulated streamflow in the upper Delaware River Basin.

June 7, 2004, marked the 50th anniversary of the Amended Decree of the Supreme Court of the United States that allocated the waters of the Delaware River Basin and established the Office of the Delaware River Master. A congressional briefing in Washington, D.C., hosted by the U.S. Geological Survey (USGS), commemorated this milestone.

The USGS continued operation of its field office of the Delaware River Master at Milford, Pennsylvania. Gary N. Paulachok, Deputy Delaware River Master, continued in charge of the office, assisted by Bruce E. Krejmas, Hydrologist.

During the year, the River Master's office continued the weekly distribution of a summary hydrologic report. These reports contain provisional data on precipitation in the upper Delaware River Basin, releases and spills from New York City reservoirs to the Delaware River, diversions to the New York City water-supply system, reservoir contents, daily segregation of flow of the Delaware River at the USGS Montague, New Jersey, gaging station, and diversions by New Jersey. The reports were distributed to members of the Delaware River Master Advisory Committee and to other parties interested in Delaware River operations. A monthly summary of hydrologic conditions also was provided to Advisory Committee members.

The first section of this report documents Delaware River operations during the report year. During the year, the City of New York diverted 196.110 Bgal from the Delaware River Basin and released 99.441 Bgal from Pepacton, Cannonsville, and Neversink Reservoirs to the Delaware River. The River Master directed releases from these reservoirs to the Delaware River that totaled 10.628 Bgal.

The second section of this report describes water quality at various monitor sites on the Delaware Estuary. It includes basic data on chemical properties and physical characteristics of the water and presents summary statistics on the data.

Throughout the year, diversions to New York City's water supply and releases designed to maintain the flow of the Delaware River at Montague were made as directed by the River Master. Diversions by New York City from its reservoirs in the Delaware River Basin did not exceed the limit stipulated by the Decree. Diversions by New Jersey also were within the stipulated limit.

The River Master and staff are grateful for the continued cooperation and support of the Parties to the Decree. Also, the contributions of the PPL Corporation and Mirant Corporation in informing the River Master of plans for power generation and furnishing data on reservoir releases are greatly appreciated.

Sincerely yours,

/Signed/

Stephen F. Blanchard
Delaware River Master

DELAWARE RIVER OPERATIONS

Abstract

A Decree of the Supreme Court of the United States, entered in 1954, established the position of Delaware River Master within the U.S. Geological Survey (USGS). In addition, the Decree authorizes diversions of water from the Delaware River Basin and requires compensating releases from certain reservoirs, owned by New York City, to be made under the supervision and direction of the River Master. The Decree stipulates that the River Master will furnish reports to the Court, not less frequently than annually. This report is the 51st Annual Report of the River Master of the Delaware River. It covers the 2004 River Master report year; that is, the period from December 1, 2003, to November 30, 2004.

During the report year, precipitation in the upper Delaware River Basin was 9.03 in. (121 percent) greater than the long-term average. Combined storage in Pepacton, Cannonsville, and Neversink Reservoirs was at a record high level on December 1, 2003. Reservoir storage remained high throughout the year with at least one reservoir spilling every month of the year. Delaware River operations throughout the year were conducted as stipulated by the Decree.

Diversions from the Delaware River Basin by New York City and New Jersey were in compliance with the Decree. Reservoir releases were made as directed by the River Master at rates designed to meet the flow objective for the Delaware River at Montague, New Jersey, on 30 days during the report year. Releases were made at conservation rates—or rates designed to relieve thermal stress and protect the fishery and aquatic habitat in the tailwaters of the reservoirs—on all other days.

During the report year, New York City and New Jersey complied fully with the terms of the Decree, and directives and requests of the River Master.

As part of a long-term program, the quality of water in the Delaware Estuary between Trenton, New Jersey, and Reedy Island Jetty, Delaware, was monitored at various locations. Data on water temperature, specific conductance, dissolved oxygen, and pH were collected continuously by electronic instruments at four sites. In addition, selected water-quality data were collected at 3 sites on a monthly basis and at 19 sites on a semi-monthly basis.

Introduction

An Amended Decree of the Supreme Court of the United States, entered June 7, 1954, authorized diversions of water from the Delaware River Basin and provided for releases of water from three New York City reservoirs to the upper Delaware River. The Decree stipulated that these diversions and releases were to be made under the supervision and direction of the Delaware River Master. The Decree also stipulated that reports on Delaware River operations be made to the Court not less frequently than annually. This report documents operations from December 1, 2003, to November 30, 2004, or the 2004 River Master report year. The report also presents information on the quality of water in the Delaware Estuary during the report year.

Some hydrologic data presented in this report are records of streamflow and water quality for USGS data-collection stations. These records were collected, computed, and furnished by the offices of the USGS at Troy, New York; Exton and New Cumberland, Pennsylvania; and West Trenton, New Jersey, in cooperation with the States of New York and New Jersey, the Commonwealth of Pennsylvania, and the City of New York. The locations of major streams and reservoirs, and selected streamflow-gaging stations in the Delaware River Basin are shown in figure 1.

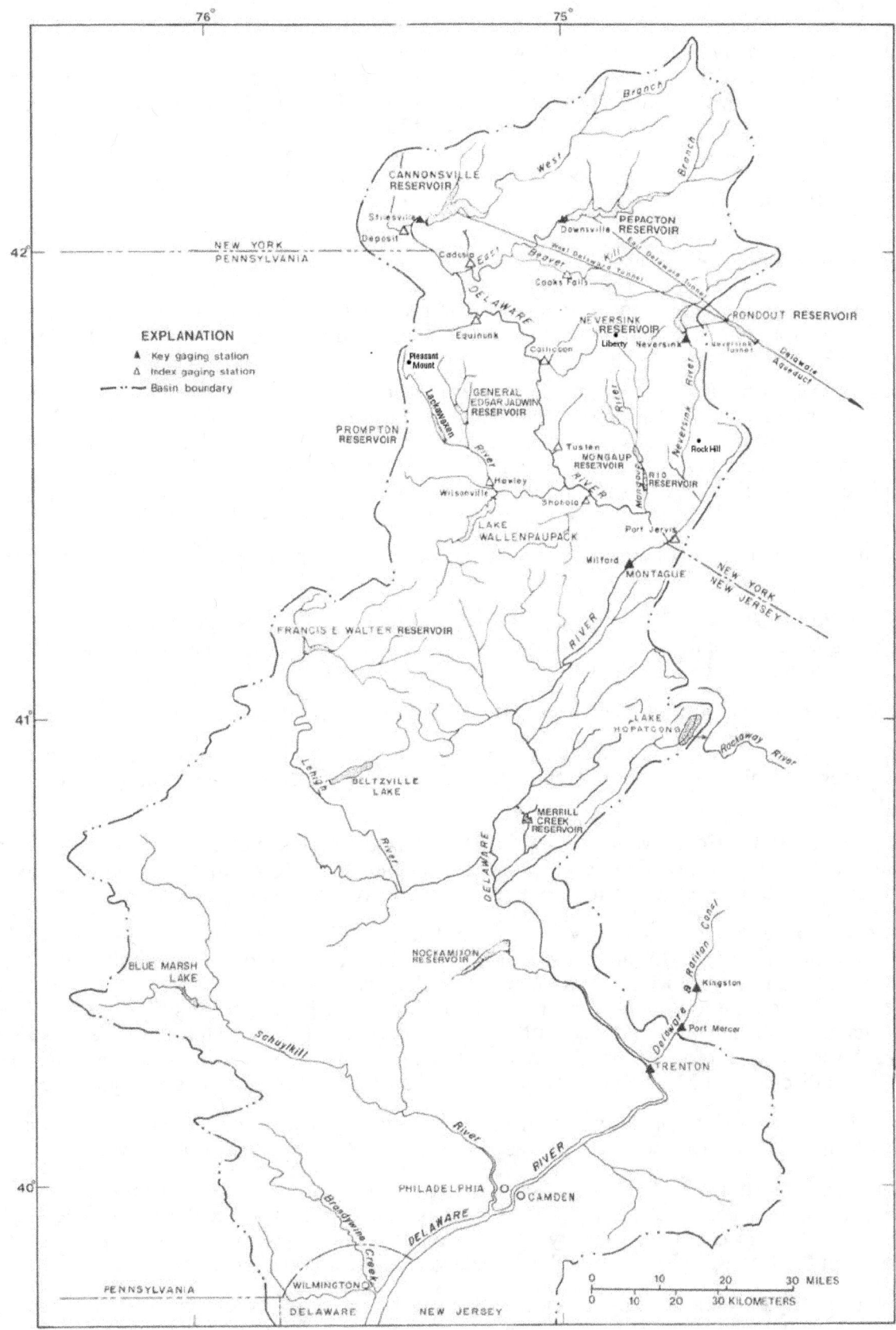

Figure 1. Delaware River Basin above Wilmington, Delaware.

5

Acknowledgments

The River Master's daily operation records were prepared from hydrologic data collected chiefly on a day-to-day basis. Data for these records were collected and computed by the Office of the Delaware River Master or were furnished by the following agencies and utilities: Data for Pepacton, Cannonsville, and Neversink Reservoirs by the New York City Department of Environmental Protection, Bureau of Water Supply; for Lake Wallenpaupack by the PPL Corporation; and for Rio Reservoir by Mirant Corporation. Precipitation data and quantitative precipitation forecasts were provided by the National Weather Service (NWS) office in Binghamton, New York.

Definition of Terms and Procedures

The following definitions apply to various terms and procedures used in the operations documented in this report. A table for converting inch-pound units to the International System of Units (SI) is given on page vi.

- **Balancing Adjustment.**—An operating procedure to correct for inaccuracies inherent in the design of releases from New York City reservoirs to meet the Montague flow objective. The balancing adjustment is computed as 10 percent of the difference between the cumulative adjusted directed release and the cumulative directed release required for exact forecasting. The balancing adjustment is applied to the following day's release design. The maximum daily balancing adjustment is purposely limited to preclude unacceptably large variations in the adjusted flow objective.

- **Capacity.**—Total usable volume in a reservoir between the point of maximum depletion and the elevation of the lowest crest of the spillway.

- **Conservation releases.**—Controlled releases from Pepacton, Cannonsville, and Neversink Reservoirs designed to maintain specified minimum flows in stream channels below the reservoirs. The conservation rates shown in table 2 are defined as follows:

  - **Basic.**—Conservation release rates in effect prior to 1977.

  - **Augmented.**—Conservation releases at rates greater than basic, designed to protect and enhance the recreational use of waters affected by such releases. These releases initially went into effect in 1977.

  - **Experimental.**—Conservation releases that are based on the same total quantity of water as the augmented conservation releases, plus any applicable thermal stress-relief water, and designed to meet the specific needs of various experimental reservoir releases programs since 1983.

- **Daily excess-release credits.**—Daily credits and deficits during the seasonal release period (June 15 to the following March 15) are computed as the arithmetic difference between the daily mean discharge of the Delaware River at Montague, New Jersey, and 1,750 ft³/s. The daily credit cannot exceed the 24-hour period releases from Pepacton, Cannonsville, and Neversink Reservoirs routed to Montague and made in accordance with direction, except as follows: during the seasonal period, credits also are applied for part or all of other releases from these reservoirs that contribute to the daily mean discharge at Montague between 1,750 ft³/s and the applicable excess-release rate.

- **Directed releases.**—Controlled releases from New York City reservoirs in the upper Delaware River Basin, designed by the Delaware River Master to meet the Montague flow objective.

- **Diversions.**—The transfer of water by New York City from Pepacton, Cannonsville, and Neversink Reservoirs in the upper Delaware River Basin through the East Delaware, West Delaware, and Neversink Tunnels, respectively, to the City's water-supply system. Also, the transfer of water by New Jersey from the Delaware River through the Delaware and Raritan Canal.

- **Excess quantity.**—As defined by the Decree, the excess quantity of water is equal to 83 percent of the amount by which the estimated consumption in New York City during the year is less than the City's estimate of continuous safe yield (1,665 Mgal/d stipulated by the 1954 Decree) from all its sources of supply obtainable without pumping, except that the excess quantity shall not exceed 70 billion gallons. Each year, the seasonal period for release of the excess quantity begins on June 15. The flow objective for the period becomes effective at Montague on that date and remains in effect until the following March 15, or until the cumulative total of excess-release credits equals the applicable excess quantity, whichever occurs first.

- **Index gaging stations.**—Particular sites on tributaries of the upper Delaware River where systematic observations of gage height and discharge are made. These stations are used mainly during the directed-release season to estimate inflows of surface water to the upper Delaware River.

- **Key gaging stations.**—Particular sites on the East Branch Delaware River, West Branch Delaware River, Neversink River, Delaware and Raritan Canal, and mainstem Delaware River where continuous, systematic observations of gage height and discharge are made. These stations are used on a year-round basis in River Master operations.

- **Maximum reservoir depletion.**—The minimum water surface level or elevation below which a reservoir ceases to continue to make delivery of quantities of water for all purposes for which the reservoir was designed. Sometimes this is referred to as minimum full-operating level.

- **Rate of flow.**—Mean discharge for a specified 24-hour period, in cubic feet per second or million gallons per day.

- **Rate of flow at Montague.**—Daily mean discharge of the Delaware River at Montague, New Jersey, computed on a calendar-day basis.

- **Reservoir-controlled releases.**—Controlled releases from reservoirs passed through outlet valves in the dams or through turbines in powerplants. These releases do not include spillway overflow at the reservoirs.

- **Storage or contents.**—Usable volume of water in a reservoir. Unless otherwise indicated, volume is computed on the basis of level pool and above the point of maximum depletion.

- **Time of day.**—Time of day is expressed in 24-hour Eastern Standard Time, which during the report year included a 23-hour day on April 4 and a 25-hour day on October 31.

- **Uncontrolled runoff at Montague.**—Runoff from the 3,480 square mile drainage area above Montague, New Jersey, excluding the drainage area above Pepacton, Cannonsville, Neversink, Wallenpaupack, and Rio Dams, but including spillway overflow at these dams.

Precipitation

Precipitation in the Delaware River Basin above Montague, New Jersey, totaled 52.42 in. during the 2004 report year and was 9.03 in. (121 percent) greater than the long-term (63-year) average. Monthly precipitation ranged from 53 percent of the long-term average in February 2004 to 238 percent of average in September 2004. Data on monthly precipitation during the report year and long-term average precipitation are presented in table 1[1]. These data were computed from records collected at 10 geographically distributed stations by the NWS; the New York City Department of Environmental Protection, Bureau of Water Supply; and the River Master office.

The seasonal period from December to May typically is when surface-water and ground-water reservoirs refill. During this period in 2003–2004, average precipitation at the 10 stations was 19.78 in., which is 98 percent of the 63-year average. During June to November, average precipitation at the 10 stations was 32.64 in., which is 141 percent of the long-term average. The maximum monthly precipitation was 11.60 inches in September 2004, measured at Pleasant Mount, Pennsylvania; the minimum monthly precipitation was 0.88 inches in February 2004, measured at Downsville, New York (locations shown on fig. 1).

---

[1]All numbered tables in the section "Delaware River Operations" are grouped at the end of this section, beginning on page 22.

Operations

December to May

Operations on December 1, 2003, were conducted as prescribed by the Decree. The Montague flow objective was 1,810 ft³/s, and the allowable diversions to New York City and New Jersey were 800 Mgal/d and 100 Mgal/d, respectively. Conservation releases from New York City reservoirs were made at the experimental release rates shown in table 2 until April 30, 2004.

From December 2003 to May 2004, the first half of the report year, total precipitation was 0.49 in. below average. Monthly precipitation ranged from 53 percent of the long-term average in February 2004 to 145 percent in December 2003 (table 1). Runoff in the upper basin was above normal in December, normal in January, March, and May, and below normal in February and April.

On December 1, 2003, when the 2004 report year began, Pepacton Reservoir contained 141.894 Bgal of water in storage above the point of maximum depletion, or 101.2 percent of the 140.190 Bgal storage capacity. Cannonsville Reservoir contained 98.088 Bgal, or 102.5 percent of the 95.706 Bgal storage capacity. Neversink Reservoir contained 34.729 Bgal, or 99.4 percent of the 34.941 Bgal storage capacity. Combined storage in these reservoirs on December 1 was 274.711 Bgal, or 101.4 percent of combined capacity. Daily storage in Pepacton, Cannonsville, and Neversink Reservoirs is shown in tables 3, 4, and 5, respectively, and combined storage during the report year is illustrated in figure 2.

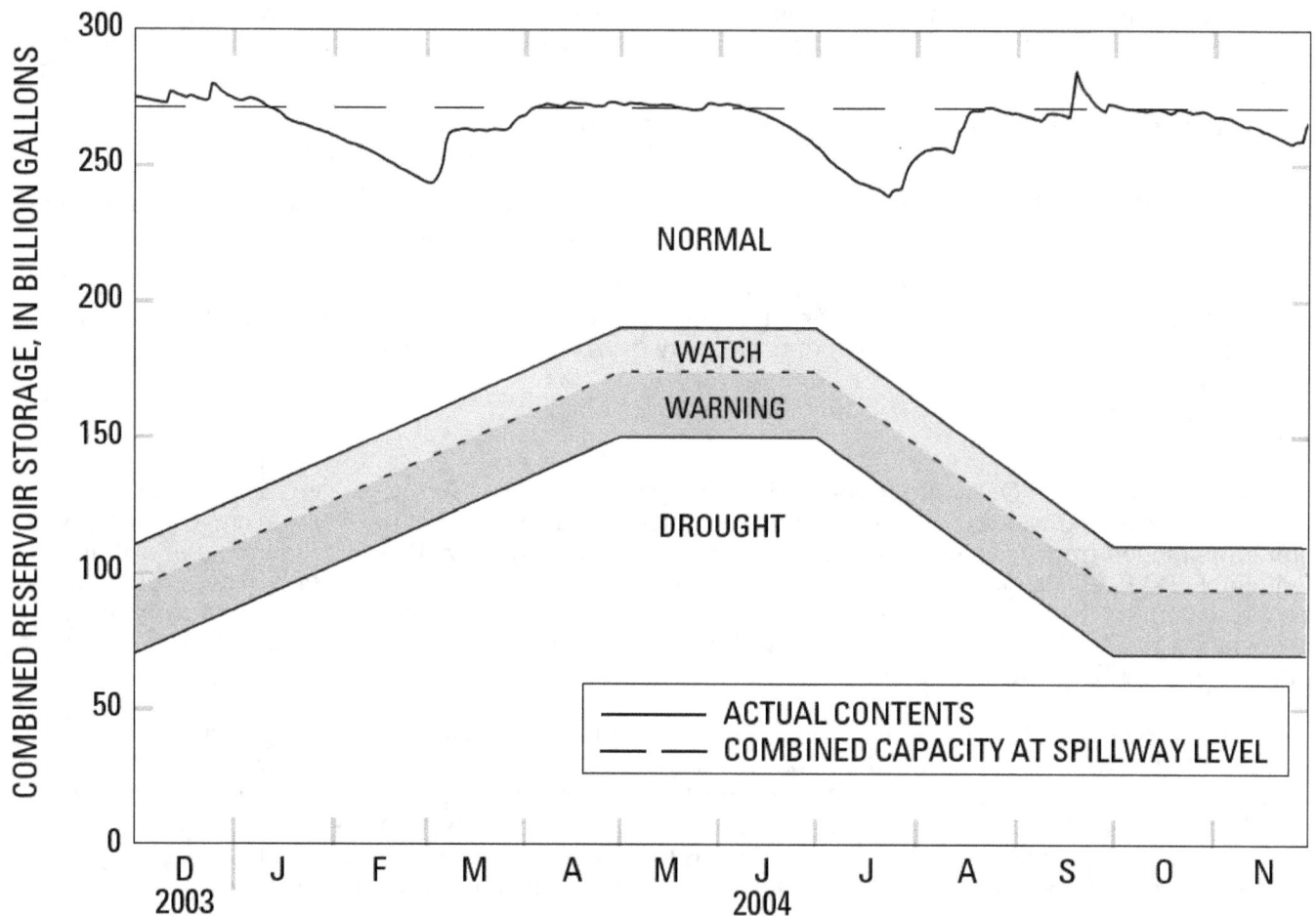

Figure 2. Operation curves and actual contents for New York City reservoirs in the Delaware River Basin, December 1, 2003, to November 30, 2004.

On December 11, 2003, in consideration of the high storage level of Pepacton Reservoir, the Decree Parties implemented a temporary spill reduction program. The program was an attempt to create a storage void, not to exceed 5 Bgal, through supplemental releases. The agreement for a temporary spill reduction program for Pepacton Reservoir is presented in Appendix A. On February 5, 2004, the temporary spill reduction program for Pepacton Reservoir was revised by the Decree Parties and extended until March 15, 2004. The agreement for the revised program is presented in Appendix B.

On April 21, 2004, the Decree Parties established an experimental augmented conservation releases program for the New York City Delaware Basin Reservoirs for the period May 1, 2004, to May 31, 2007. This program established a habitat protection bank, which consisted of an excess release quantity bank, a thermal bank, and a supplemental release bank. It also established flow targets for all three tailwaters at certain USGS gaging stations downstream of the reservoirs. The program, DRBC Docket No. D-77-20 CP (Revision 7), is presented in Appendix C.

From December to May, inflow to the City's reservoirs typically exceeds outflow and, consequently, storage increases. The average inflow to Pepacton, Cannonsville, and Neversink Reservoirs for these 6 months during the 63-year period from December 1940 to May 2003 was 301.3 Bgal. During the corresponding 6 months of the report year, inflow to the three reservoirs totaled 297.6 Bgal. Evaporation loss is not included in the computations.

Combined storage remained high and fluctuated only slightly in December 2003 and January 2004. Winter precipitation was slightly below normal and combined storage decreased slowly during February, then increased to near full capacity from March to May. The combined storage of the reservoirs was about 101 percent of capacity on May 31, 2004.

Combined storage in the three New York City reservoirs was 275.180 Bgal on November 30, 2003, and 272.284 Bgal on May 31, 2004, a net decrease of 2.896 Bgal or 1.1 percent of total capacity. The maximum combined storage from December to May was 279.616 Bgal on December 25, 2003. Maximum storage in Pepacton Reservoir during the December to May period was 143.480 Bgal on December 25; maximum storage in Cannonsville Reservoir was 101.162 Bgal on December 26; and maximum storage in Neversink Reservoir was 35.538 Bgal on December 25, 2003. Pepacton Reservoir spilled from December 1 to January 8, April 5 to May 20, and May 26–31. Cannonsville Reservoir spilled from December 1 to January 24, and March 6 to May 31. Neversink Reservoir spilled from December 1–30 and January 2 to March 4. The total spill volume during this period was 159.637 Bgal.

During the December to May period, diversions to Rondout Reservoir by New York City totaled 100.990 Bgal (552 Mgal/d). The forecasted discharge at Montague, exclusive of water released from the City reservoirs, was greater than the flow objective on all days in the period, and no releases were directed. The observed daily mean discharge at Montague was greater than the applicable flow objective on all days. Applicable design rates for the USGS gaging station Delaware River at Montague, New Jersey, are presented in table 6.

June to November

Monthly precipitation from June to November was above average in July, August, and September and below average in June, October, and November. Total precipitation during the period was 32.64 in. or 9.52 in. more than the 63-year average (table 1).

Combined storage in the three New York City reservoirs was 272.169 Bgal on June 1, 2004, and 266.335 Bgal on November 30, 2004, a net decrease of 5.834 Bgal or about 2.2 percent of total capacity. During the June to November period, maximum storage in Pepacton Reservoir was 145.152 Bgal on September 19; 104.145 Bgal in Cannonsville Reservoir on September 19; and 35.409 Bgal in Neversink Reservoir on September 19. Maximum combined storage in the three reservoirs was 284.706 Bgal on September 19, 2004. The total spill volume during this period was 75.073 Bgal.

Releases were directed to meet the Montague flow objective on 30 days between June 1 and November 30, 2004, when the forecasted discharge at Montague, exclusive of water released from the New York City reservoirs, was less than the flow objective. Releases at experimental conservation rates or at rates designed to protect the fishery and aquatic habitat were made at other times during the period.

From June 1 to June 14, the Montague flow objective was 1,750 ft³/s. The forecasted flow, exclusive of releases from Pepacton, Cannonsville, and Neversink Reservoirs, did not fall below the flow objective and no releases were directed.

The New York City Department of Environmental Protection, Bureau of Water Supply, Quality, and Protection furnished the River Master with the following data for the 2004 calendar year, as stipulated by the Decree:

1. The estimated continuous safe yield from all the City's sources, obtainable without pumping, is 1,665 Mgal/d, or a total during calendar year 2004 of 1.665 Bgal/d x 366 days = 609.390 Bgal.

2. The estimated consumption that the City must provide for, from all its sources of supply during calendar year 2004, is 591.582 + 7.250 = 598.832 Bgal.

On the basis of the Decree and the aforementioned data, the aggregate quantity of excess-release water was 83 percent of (609.390 - 598.832), or 8.763 Bgal.

Data on water consumption by the City of New York for each calendar year since 1950, from all sources of supply, are presented in table 7.

As part of the reservoir releases program described in DRBC Docket No. D-77-20 CP (Revision No. 7), about 42 percent of the annual excess-release quantity was placed in a habitat protection bank. The remainder of the excess-release quantity could be used to provide an increase in the Montague flow objective or could be banked in accordance with the procedures outlined in the DRBC's Lower Basin Drought Management Plan.

On June 15, 2004, the beginning of the seasonal excess-release period, the Montague flow objective was increased to 1,820 ft³/s. Storage in the New York City reservoirs declined slowly from June to late July, after which storage increased to nearly full or full levels through the end of the report year.

On July 13, 2004, the reservoir releases program was amended to allow a portion of the Excess Release Quantity to be used for research related to aquatic resources. The agreement for the amended program, DRBC Docket No. D-77-20 CP (Revision 8) is presented in Appendix D.

On August 17, 2004, in response to abnormally high storage levels in Pepacton and Cannonsville Reservoirs, persistent wet weather, and continuing high runoff, a temporary bottom release program was implemented by the Decree Parties to reduce the quantity of warm surface water that could spill from the reservoirs. The agreement for the temporary bottom release program is presented in Appendix E.

From September 17 to 19, 2004, the remnants of Tropical Storm Ivan caused widespread flooding in the Delaware River Basin.

Between June 15 and November 30, 2004, the forecasted flow at Montague, exclusive of releases from the New York City reservoirs, was less than the flow objective on 30 days and releases were directed. On 11 days during the June 15 to November 30 period, the observed flow was less than the flow objective. On 10 of these 11 days, observed flows were within 10 percent of the flow objective. Applicable design rates for the USGS gaging station Delaware River at Montague, New Jersey, are presented in table 6.

The total discharge measured at Montague, the portion derived from uncontrolled runoff from the drainage area below the reservoirs, the portion contributed by power reservoirs, and the portion contributed by Pepacton, Cannonsville, and Neversink Reservoirs from June to August are show in figure 3. In developing the water budget for Montague, uncontrolled runoff was computed as the residual of observed flow minus releases and spills from all reservoirs, and, consequently, was subject to errors in observations, transit times, and routing of the various components of flow. The conservation release from Rio Reservoir is included in the uncontrolled runoff component. The net effect of these uncertainties is incorporated in the computation of uncontrolled runoff. From June 1 to November 20, 2004, diversions from the three New York City Delaware Basin reservoirs to Rondout Reservoir totaled 95.120 Bgal.

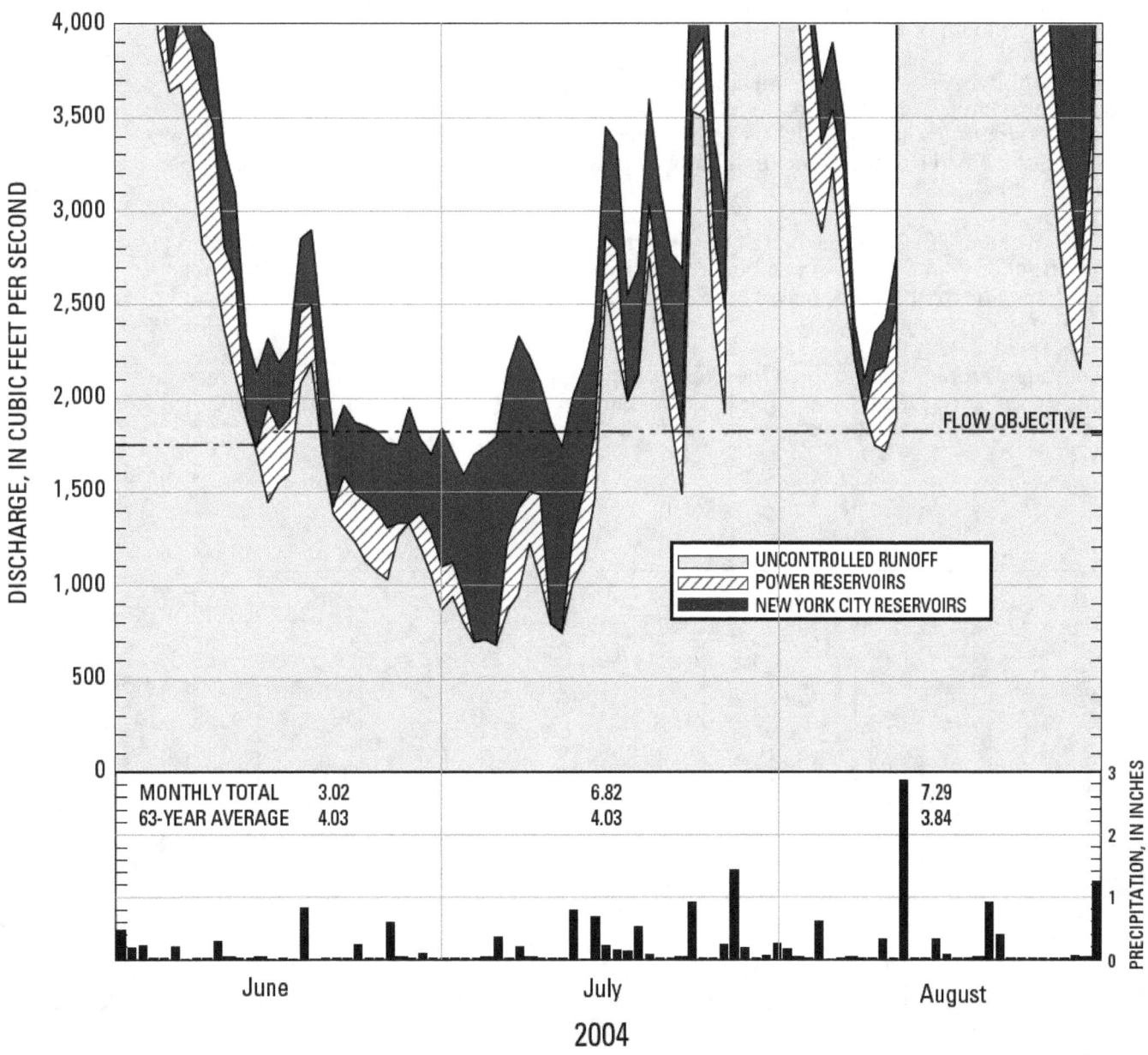

Figure 3. Components of flow, Delaware River at Montague, New Jersey, June 1 to August 31, 2004.

Summary of Operations

From December 1, 2003, to November 30, 2004, diversions from the three New York City reservoirs in the upper Delaware River Basin to Rondout Reservoir totaled 196.110 Bgal, and all releases from the three reservoirs to the Delaware River totaled 99.441 Bgal. River Master-directed releases to the Delaware River from these reservoirs totaled 10.628 Bgal.

During the year, maximum storage in Pepacton Reservoir was 145.152 Bgal on September 19, 2004; 104.145 Bgal in Cannonsville Reservoir on September 19; and 35.428 Bgal in Neversink Reservoir on December 12, 2003. Maximum combined storage in the three reservoirs was 284.706 Bgal (105.1 percent) on September 19, 2004. The total combined spill for the year was 234.710 Bgal and at least one reservoir spilled every month of the year.

During the report year, minimum storage in Pepacton Reservoir was 119.257 Bgal (85.1 percent of capacity) on March 2 and 3, 2004; 80.557 Bgal (84.2 percent of capacity) in Cannonsville Reservoir on July 26, 2004; and 28.861 Bgal (82.6 percent of capacity) in Neversink Reservoir on November 28, 2004. Minimum combined storage in the three reservoirs was 238.376 Bgal (88.0 percent of combined capacity) on July 23, 2004.

On November 30, 2004, the end of the report year, combined storage in the three reservoirs was 266.335 Bgal or 98.3 percent of combined capacity. From December 1, 2003, to November 30, 2004, the net change in combined storage was -8.845 Bgal, or a decrease equivalent to 3.3 percent of combined capacity.

Combined storage for the three reservoirs on the first day of the month was above median in all months, except July, when it was slightly below median (fig. 4). New record-high combined storage levels for the first day of the month were set in December, January, and September.

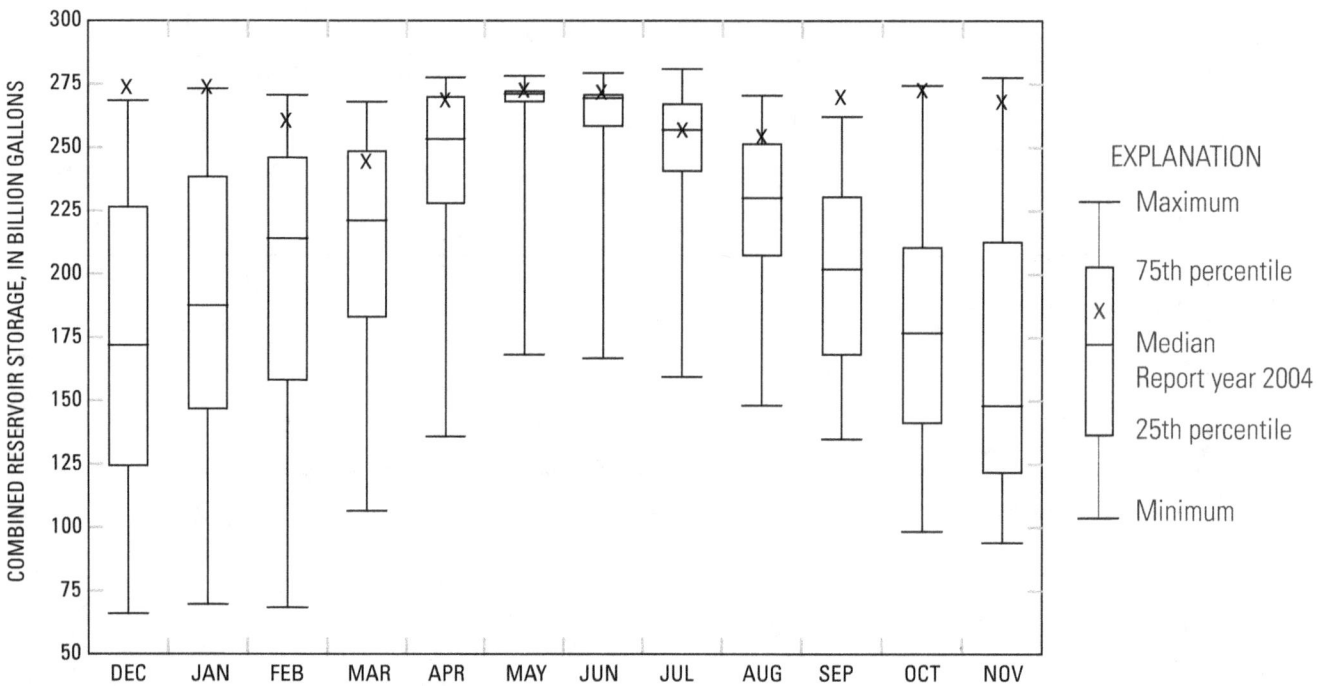

Figure 4. Combined storage in Pepacton, Cannonsville, and Neversink Reservoirs on the first day of the month, December 2003 to November 2004 (this report year), and summary statistics for the reference period, June 1967 to November 2003.

Streamflow

Components of Flow, Delaware River at Montague, New Jersey

The data and computations of the various components of flow form the basic operational records used by the River Master to carry out specific responsibilities related to the Montague formula. The operational record has two parts: forecasted flow at Montague, exclusive of controlled releases from New York City's reservoirs (table 8), and segregation of components of daily mean flow at Montague (table 9).

The following components may be present in the flow of the Delaware River at Montague:

1. Controlled releases from Lake Wallenpaupack on Wallenpaupack Creek, for the production of hydroelectric power.

2. Controlled releases from Rio Reservoir on Mongaup River, for the production of hydroelectric power.

3. Runoff from the uncontrolled area above Montague, including spills from New York City reservoirs, Lake Wallenpaupack, and Rio Reservoir.

4. Controlled releases from Pepacton, Cannonsville, and Neversink Reservoirs of New York City.

The releases from New York City's reservoirs necessary to maintain the Montague flow objective were computed on the basis of the forecasted flow at Montague, exclusive of controlled releases from the reservoirs.

Time of Travel

Following are average times for the effective travel of water from the various sources of controlled supply to Montague, New Jersey. These times were used for flow routing during the 2004 report year.

Source	Travel times, in hours
Pepacton Reservoir	60
Cannonsville Reservoir	48
Neversink Reservoir	33
Lake Wallenpaupack	16
Rio Reservoir	8

The travel times were computed from reservoir and powerplant operations data and historical streamflow records. The travel times generally are suitable for use in the operations of the River Master. Occasionally, however, significant exceptions are observed. For example, when a large release from Cannonsville Reservoir follows a small release, a substantial portion of the water fills the channel en route, and the remainder may arrive at Montague as much as 66 hours after the time of release. During winter, the formation of ice cover, together with lower streamflow, gradually increases the resistance to water flow, resulting in increased travel times. Because ice-affected travel times increase gradually over several days, and releases were not directed to meet the Montague flow objective during periods of ice cover, no adjustments were made to compensate for increased travel times during these periods of the report year.

Segregation of Flow at Montague

The River Master daily operations record of reservoir releases and segregation of the various components contributing to the flow of the Delaware River at Montague, New Jersey, are presented in table 9. The data are arranged to conform to the downstream movement of water from the various sources to Montague. Summation of data along individual rows in the table is equivalent to routing the various flow contributions to Montague, using the aforementioned average travel times. Uncontrolled runoff was computed as a residual by subtracting the flow contributions of all other sources from the observed discharge at Montague.

Computation of Directed Releases

During the report year, the River Master used the following information for daily operations: (1) discharges computed from recorded or reported stream gage heights, for various 24-hour periods, absent real-time information on any changes in stage-discharge relations; (2) daily discharge from New York City's three reservoirs, measured with venturi meters; (3) precipitation reports for the previous 24 hours; (4) actual powerplant releases converted to daily discharges; (5) advance estimates of power demand converted to daily discharges; (6) advance estimates of uncontrolled runoff at Montague; and (7) average travel times for routing water from various sources. Although uncertainty is inherent in the advance estimates, this information by necessity is used in the daily design and direction of reservoir releases.

The 60-hour travel time of water from Pepacton Reservoir to Montague is greater than the travel time of water from any other reservoir in the upper Delaware River Basin. Releases from Cannonsville and Neversink Reservoirs were timed to arrive at Montague concurrently with releases from Pepacton Reservoir. To allow for differences in travel times, daily directed releases were scheduled to begin from Pepacton Reservoir at 1200 hours, from Cannonsville Reservoir at 2400 hours, and from Neversink Reservoir at 1500 hours the following day.

Releases from the City's reservoirs required to maintain the Montague flow objective were computed from forecasts of releases from Lake Wallenpaupack and Rio Reservoir, and estimates of uncontrolled runoff at Montague. To account for the travel times from these sources to Montague, the computation requires estimates of the following components of flow two or more days in advance: (1) release of water from Lake Wallenpaupack; (2) release of water from Rio Reservoir; and (3) uncontrolled runoff at Montague. The River Master operations record for computing daily directed release requirements during periods of low flow is given in table 8.

The electric utilities furnished forecasts of power generation and releases. Because the hydroelectric plants were used chiefly for area regulation or meeting peak power demands, the forecasts were subject to various modifying factors including the vagaries of weather on electricity demand. In addition, because the power companies are members of regional power pools, demand for power outside of the local service area may unexpectedly affect generation schedules. Consequently, at times, the actual use of water for power generation differed considerably from the forecasts used in the design of reservoir releases.

For computational purposes during periods of low flow, estimates of uncontrolled runoff at Montague were treated as two components: (1) current runoff and (2) forecasted increase in runoff from precipitation. Estimates of these components are given in table 8.

During ice-free conditions, current runoff was computed using a routing and recession procedure based on discharges at 0800 hours at the following USGS gaging stations:

Station Name	Drainage Area (mi^2)
Beaver Kill at Cooks Falls, New York	241
Cadosia Creek at Cadosia, New York	17.9
Oquaga Creek at Deposit, New York	67.6
Equinunk Creek at Equinunk, Pennsylvania	56.3
Callicoon Creek at Callicoon, New York	110
Tenmile River at Tusten, New York	45.6
Lackawaxen River at Hawley, Pennsylvania	290
Shohola Creek near Shohola, Pennsylvania	83.6
Neversink River at Port Jervis, New York	336

During winter, the advance estimate of uncontrolled runoff (current conditions) was made on the basis of flows at a reduced network of gaging stations and the recession curve for computed uncontrolled flow at Montague.

The forecasted runoff from precipitation is shown in table 8 under the heading "Weather Adjustment." Throughout the year, the NWS office in Binghamton, New York, furnished quantitative forecasts of average precipitation and air temperatures for the drainage basin above Montague, New Jersey. During winter, runoff was estimated on the basis of the current status of snow and ice, along with forecasted precipitation and temperature. During other periods, forecasted precipitation was used to estimate runoff.

The forecasted flow at Montague, exclusive of releases from New York City's reservoirs (table 8), is computed as the sum of forecasted releases from power reservoirs, estimated uncontrolled runoff including conservation releases from Rio Reservoir, and weather adjustments. If the computed total flow was less than the flow objective at Montague, then the deficiency was made up by releases from the City's reservoirs, as directed by the River Master.

When forecasts of precipitation or powerplant releases were revised appreciably after a release was directed, the release required from the City's reservoirs was recomputed. Commonly, this procedure resulted in a reduced release requirement for New York City reservoirs for that day. Only final figures for releases from New York City reservoirs are given in table 8.

Analysis of Forecasts

Forecasts of streamflow at Montague, developed on the basis of anticipated contributions from the components described previously (excluding releases from New York City's reservoirs), differed on most days from observed flow. Occasionally, variations in the components were partially compensating and observed flows were in excellent agreement with forecasted flows.

The forecasted flow of the Delaware River at Montague, exclusive of releases from New York City reservoirs, was less than the flow objective on most days from June 17 to July 17, 2004. The following tabulation compares estimates of three components of flow at Montague with actual flow during this period.

Releases and Runoff	Forecasted flow [(ft^3/s)-d]	Actual flow [(ft^3/s)-d]
Power releases		
Lake Wallenpaupack	7,304	6,690
Rio Reservoir	284	185
Runoff from uncontrolled area	32,992	38,368

From June 17 to July 17, actual releases from Lake Wallenpaupack averaged 8.4 percent less than forecasted releases, and actual and forecasted releases from Rio Reservoir were 0 ft^3/s on all but 3 days. Observed runoff from the uncontrolled area was about 16 percent more than forecasted runoff.

On any given day, forecasted releases and actual releases can differ considerably. The ranges of actual daily releases from June 17 to July 17, 2004, are as follows: daily releases at Lake Wallenpaupack differed from forecasted releases by 141 ft^3/s less to 146 ft^3/s more and daily releases at Rio Reservoir differed from forecasted releases by 71 ft^3/s less to 43 ft^3/s more. On the basis of observed flows at Montague, total directed releases from New York City's reservoirs during the report year were about 13 percent more than that required for exact forecasting.

Comparison of hydrographs of forecasted daily runoff and observed daily runoff from the uncontrolled area (fig. 5) indicates that the forecasts generally were suitable for use in designing releases from New York City's reservoirs. Numerical adjustments to the designs were made when needed to compensate for errors in the forecasts, but, because of travel times, the effects of the adjustments on flows at Montague are not evident until several days after the design date.

Analysis of the precipitation forecasts shows that the total precipitation amount forecasted for the 3-day design periods is reasonably accurate, but often the actual timing of precipitation events may be earlier or later than forecasted. The accuracy of the runoff forecasts is affected greatly by the timing of precipitation events. In addition, if the actual storm track differs from the forecasted track, the amount and timing of runoff can be substantially different than predicted.

Diversions to New York City Water Supply

The 1954 Amended Decree authorizes New York City to divert water from the Delaware River Basin at a rate not to exceed the equivalent of 800 Mgal/d. The Decree specifies that the diversion rate shall be computed as the aggregate total diversion beginning June 1 of each year divided by the number of days elapsed since the preceding May 31.

Daily diversions during the report year from Pepacton, Cannonsville, and Neversink Reservoirs to the New York City water-supply system (Rondout Reservoir) are given in table 10. A running account of the average rates of combined diversions from the three reservoirs, computed as prescribed by the Decree, also is shown. The following tabulation shows allowable maximum diversion rates and average actual diversions for various periods during the report year.

Effective dates	Allowable diversion (Mgal/d)	Average actual diversion (Mgal/d)
December 1, 2003, to May 31, 2004	800	552
June 1 to November 30, 2004	800	520

During the report year, a total of 196.110 Bgal of water was diverted to the New York City water-supply system. The allowable diversion was 345.595 Bgal.

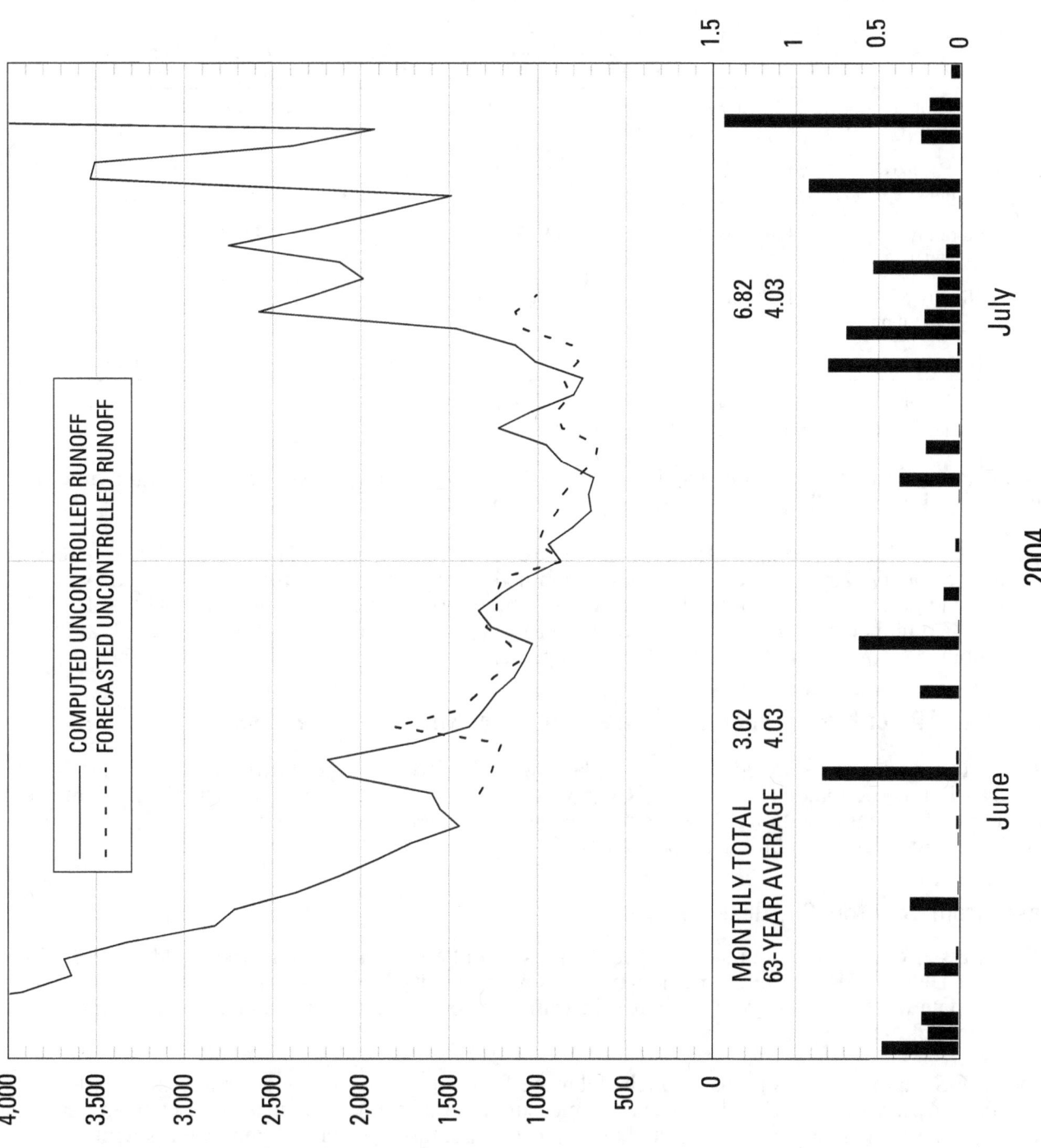

Figure 5. Uncontrolled runoff component, Delaware River at Montague, New Jersey, June 1 to July 31, 2004.

17

Storage in New York City Reservoirs

The following tabulation summarizes the "point of maximum depletion" and other pertinent levels and contents of Pepacton, Cannonsville, and Neversink Reservoirs. This information was provided by the New York City Board of Water Supply.

Level	Pepacton Reservoir		Cannonsville Reservoir		Neversink Reservoir	
	Elevation (ft)	Contents (Bgal)	Elevation (ft)	Contents (Bgal)	Elevation (ft)	Contents (Bgal)
Full pool or spillway crest	1,280.00	*140.190	1,150.00	*95.706	1,440.00	*34.941
Point of maximum depletion	1,152.00	*3.511	1,040.00	*1.020	1,319.00	*0.525
Sill of diversion tunnel	1,143.00	*4.200	+1,035.00	*1.564	1,314.00	
Sill of river outlet tunnel	1,126.50		1,020.50		1,314.00	
Dead storage		1.800		0.328		1.680

*Contents shown are quantities stored between listed elevations.

+Elevation of mouth of inlet channel of diversion works.

Daily storage in Pepacton, Cannonsville, and Neversink Reservoirs, above the "point of maximum depletion" or minimum full-operating level, is given in tables 3, 4, and 5.

On December 1, 2003, combined storage in the three reservoirs was 274.711 Bgal, or 101.4 percent of combined capacity. As discussed previously, combined storage remained high throughout the year and never declined below 88 percent of total capacity. The three reservoirs spilled a total of 234.710 Bgal during the year. Combined storage reached a maximum for the report year on September 19, 2004, at 284.706 Bgal. Combined storage was 266.335 Bgal, or 98.3 percent of combined capacity, on November 30, 2004.

Comparison of River Master Operations Data With Other Streamflow Records

River Master operations are conducted on a day-to-day basis and, by necessity, use preliminary data on streamflow. In this section, records used in River Master operations are compared to final data published for selected USGS gaging stations. Data on releases were reported in million gallons per day and converted to cubic feet per second for use in the comparisons.

Releases from New York City Reservoirs

River Master operations data on controlled releases from Pepacton, Cannonsville, and Neversink Reservoirs to the Delaware River were furnished by the New York City Department of Environmental Protection. These data were obtained from calibrated instruments connected to venturi meters installed in the outlet conduits of the reservoirs.

The USGS gaging station on East Branch Delaware River at Downsville, New York, is 0.5 mile downstream from Downsville Dam (fig. 1). Discharge measured at this station includes releases from Pepacton Reservoir and a small amount of seepage and any runoff that enters the channel between the dam and the gaging station. The drainage area is 371 mi^2 at the dam and 372 mi^2 at the gaging station.

The following tabulation compares releases from Pepacton Reservoir (table 9), reported by New York City, to the final records for the USGS gaging station on East Branch Delaware River at Downsville, New York (table 11), for the flow objectives shown.

	35	45
Flow objective (ft³/s)	35	45
Number of USGS daily mean discharge values used in comparison	13	57
New York City-measured mean flow (ft³/s)	35.6	44.8
USGS-computed mean flow (ft³/s)	41.4	39.9
Percent difference	-14.0	+12.3

The differences at the two flow rates are less than 15 percent. The instruments connected to the venturi meters were recalibrated periodically by New York City to improve the accuracy of the recorded flow data.

The USGS gaging station on West Branch Delaware River at Stilesville, New York, is 1.4 miles downstream from Cannonsville Dam (fig. 1). Discharge measured at this station includes releases from Cannonsville Reservoir and runoff from 2 mi² of drainage area between the dam and the gaging station. The drainage area is 454 mi² at the dam and 456 mi² at the gaging station. The gaging-station records are rated fair at flows greater than 100 ft³/s and poor at flows less than 100 ft³/s. A rating of "fair" means that about 95 percent of the daily discharges are within 15 percent of the true discharge, whereas a rating of "poor" means that daily discharges have less than "fair" accuracy. The records include runoff from the area between the dam and the gaging station, and seepage near the base of the dam. The final discharge record for the USGS gaging station on West Branch Delaware River at Stilesville, New York, is presented in table 12.

The USGS gaging station on Neversink River at Neversink, New York, is 1,650 ft downstream from Neversink Dam (fig. 1). Discharge measured at this station includes releases from Neversink Reservoir and, during storms, a small amount of runoff that originates between the dam and the gaging station. The drainage area is 92.5 mi² at the dam and 92.6 mi² at the gaging station.

The following tabulation compares releases from Neversink Reservoir (table 9), reported by New York City, to the final records for the USGS gaging station on Neversink River at Neversink, New York (table 13), for the flow objective shown.

Flow objective (ft³/s)	25
Number of USGS daily mean discharge values used in comparison	112
New York City-measured mean flow (ft³/s)	24.8
USGS-computed mean flow (ft³/s)	24.3
Percent difference	+2.1

Releases from Lake Wallenpaupack

Records of daily discharge through the Wallenpaupack powerplant were furnished by the PPL Corporation and published by the USGS as Wallenpaupack Creek at Wilsonville, Pennsylvania (table 14). These discharges represent the flow through the turbines of the powerplant and were computed on a midnight-to-midnight basis. For River Master operations, flows were computed on a 24-hour basis beginning at 0800 hours to compensate for the 16-hour travel time to Montague, New Jersey (table 9).

From December 2003 to November 2004, the River Master's record agrees with the published USGS record except for some very small differences that result mainly from differences in timeframe and rounding of computations. Overall, the records agree to within 0.2 percent for the year.

Delaware River at Montague, New Jersey

The River Master's operations record for the Delaware River at Montague, New Jersey (table 9), showed 0.3 percent more discharge for the report year than the published USGS record for the gaging station (table 15). Daily values for the two records were in good agreement, except during ice-affected periods.

Diversion Tunnels

Records of diversions through the East Delaware, West Delaware, and Neversink Tunnels (fig. 1) were furnished by the New York City Department of Environmental Protection. These records were obtained from the City's calibrated instruments connected to venturi meters installed in the tunnel conduits. The measured flows were transmitted electronically on a 15-second interval to a City computer and, on 5-minute intervals, release and diversion quantities for the preceding 5-minute period were computed using the instantaneous rate-of-flow data from each instrument. These 5-minute quantities were then summed to compute daily total flows, which were reported to the River Master's office on a daily basis. On a weekly basis, the diversion figures were checked against the flow meter totalizer readings and corrected when necessary.

The East Delaware Tunnel is used to divert water from Pepacton Reservoir to Rondout Reservoir. Conditions in the outlet channel of the East Delaware Tunnel were unfavorable for flow measurements during the report year because of high water levels in Rondout Reservoir.

The generating plant at the downstream end of the East Delaware Tunnel operated most days of the report year. When the powerplant was not in operation, some water leaked through the wicket gates and was not recorded on the totalizer. A current-meter measurement made in 1989 shows that the (assumed constant) rate of leakage is about 8.0 Mgal/d. Because the powerplant was not in operation for the equivalent of 109 days during the 2004 report year, the unmeasured leakage was estimated to be about 0.9 Bgal.

The West Delaware Tunnel is used to divert water from Cannonsville Reservoir to Rondout Reservoir. Inspections of the channel below the outlet, when valves were closed, revealed only negligible leakage. A hydroelectric powerplant uses water diverted through the West Delaware Tunnel, but the plant operates only when diversions are less than 300 Mgal/d. When the powerplant is not operating, the valves on the pipelines to the plant are closed, and there is no leakage through the system.

The Neversink Tunnel is used to divert water from Neversink Reservoir to Rondout Reservoir. A hydroelectric powerplant uses water diverted through the Neversink Tunnel. When the powerplant is not operating and the main valve on the diversion tunnel is open, leakage develops that is not recorded on the venturi instruments. One current-meter measurement made in 1999 showed a leakage rate of 16.2 ft^3/s (10.5 Mgal/d). When the powerplant is operating, the leakage is included in the recorded flow. No leakage occurs when the main valve on the tunnel is closed. During the 2004 report year, the powerplant operated part of the day on most days and was not operated the equivalent of 211 days. Using the leakage rate noted above and records of powerplant operation, about 2.2 Bgal of water was diverted but not recorded.

Diversions by New Jersey

The Amended Decree authorizes New Jersey to divert water from the Delaware River and its tributaries in New Jersey, to areas outside the Delaware River Basin, without compensating releases. These diversions may not exceed 100 Mgal/d as a monthly average, and the daily mean diversion may not exceed 120 Mgal/d. The USGS gaging station on Delaware and Raritan Canal at Port Mercer, New Jersey (fig. 1), is used as the official control point for measuring diversions by New Jersey (table 16).

The following tabulation gives the allowable diversion by New Jersey, the period it was in effect, and the maximum monthly diversion during the report year.

Effective dates	Allowable monthly average diversion (Mgal/d)	Maximum monthly average diversion (Mgal/d)	Month of maximum average diversion
Dec. 1, 2003, to Nov. 30, 2004	100	94.6	January

The maximum daily mean diversion was 103 Mgal on January 25, 26, and 28, 2004. Diversions by New Jersey did not exceed the limits prescribed by the Decree.

Conformance of Operations Under the Amended Decree of the U.S. Supreme Court Entered June 7, 1954

From December 1, 2003, to November 30, 2004, operations of the Delaware River Master were conducted as stipulated by the Decree.

Diversions from the Delaware River Basin to the New York City water-supply system did not exceed those authorized by the Decree. Under compensating releases of the Montague Formula, New York City released water from its reservoirs at rates designed by the River Master to maintain the applicable flow objectives at Montague, New Jersey. During the report year, New York City complied fully with all directives and requests of the River Master.

Diversions from the Delaware River Basin by New Jersey were within limits stipulated by the Decree. New Jersey complied fully with all directives and requests of the River Master.

Table 1. Precipitation in the Delaware River Basin above Montague, New Jersey.

[All values, except percentages, in inches]

Month	December 1940 to November 2003 Monthly Average	December 2003 to November 2004			
		Amount	Percent of average	Excess (+) or deficit (-)	
				Month	Cumulative
December	3.37	4.90	145	+1.53	+1.53
January	2.98	2.60	87	-.38	+1.15
February	2.64	1.41	53	-1.23	-.08
March	3.35	2.22	66	-1.13	-1.21
April	3.72	3.84	103	+.12	-1.09
May	4.21	4.81	114	+.60	-.49
June	4.03	3.02	75	-1.01	-1.50
July	4.03	6.82	169	+2.79	+1.29
August	3.84	7.29	190	+3.45	+4.74
September	3.99	9.50	238	+5.51	+10.25
October	3.43	2.45	71	-.98	+9.27
November	3.80	3.56	94	-.24	+9.03
12 months	43.39	52.42	121		

Table 2. Conservation release rates for New York City reservoirs in the Delaware River Basin.

[All values in cubic feet per second]

Reservoir	Effective dates	Conservation release rates		
		Basic	Augmented	Experimental
Pepacton	December 1 to March 31	6	50	45
	April 1–7	6	70	45
	April 8–30	19	70	45
	May 1–31	19	70	70
	June 1 to August 31	19	70	95
	September 1–30	19	70	70
	October 1–31	19	70	45
	November 1–30	6	50	45
Cannonsville	December 1 to March 31	8	33	45
	April 1–15	8	45	45
	April 16 to May 31	23	45	45
	June 1–14	23	45	160
	June 15 to August 15	23	325	160
	August 16 to September 15	23	45	160
	September 16 to October 31	23	45	45
	November 1–30	23	33	45
Neversink	December 1 to March 31	5	25	25
	April 1–7	5	45	25
	April 8–30	15	45	25
	May 1 to September 30	15	45	53
	October 1–31	15	45	25
	November 1–30	5	25	25

Table 3. Storage in Pepacton Reservoir, New York, for year ending November 30, 2004.
(River Master daily operations record; gage reading at 0800 hours)

[Storage in millions of gallons above elevation 1,152.00 ft. Add 7,711 million gallons for total contents above sill of outlet tunnel, elevation 1,126.50 ft. Storage at spillway level is 140,190 million gallons]

DAY	DEC	JAN	FEB	MAR	APR	MAY	JUNE	JULY	AUG	SEPT	OCT	NOV
1	141,894	141,098	130,652	119,614	137,564	140,931	140,542	133,797	131,434	139,400	141,227	138,443
2	141,486	140,690	130,387	119,257	138,443	140,727	140,672	133,455	131,915	139,087	141,079	138,517
3	141,245	140,375	129,908	119,257	139,087	140,820	140,653	133,042	132,361	138,921	140,987	138,645
4	140,913	140,393	129,625	119,614	139,547	140,820	140,579	132,486	132,594	138,829	140,857	138,682
5	140,801	140,560	129,113	120,310	139,932	140,764	140,356	131,951	132,755	138,756	140,709	138,609
6	140,672	140,690	128,813	121,882	140,301	140,764	140,301	131,630	132,916	138,627	140,616	138,461
7	140,579	140,579	128,620	125,036	140,709	140,690	140,282	131,113	132,791	138,517	140,449	138,205
8	140,486	140,375	128,269	127,128	140,950	140,634	140,098	130,848	133,024	138,314	140,024	137,930
9	140,356	139,840	127,917	128,532	140,801	140,523	139,969	130,528	133,168	138,682	139,785	137,583
10	140,264	139,381	127,548	129,447	140,634	140,375	139,877	130,138	133,204	139,069	139,601	137,218
11	140,282	138,793	127,198	130,387	140,505	140,301	139,822	129,819	132,916	139,363	139,510	136,890
12	141,839	138,314	126,813	131,273	140,393	140,264	139,693	129,483	132,701	139,565	139,656	136,617
13	141,727	137,894	126,325	131,915	140,449	140,319	139,528	129,165	134,606	139,693	139,748	136,218
14	141,412	137,328	125,940	132,486	140,653	140,634	139,289	128,813	136,981	139,767	139,822	135,892
15	141,394	136,781	125,522	132,540	140,913	140,616	139,069	128,673	138,186	139,693	139,712	135,493
16	141,134	136,073	125,122	132,773	141,005	140,653	138,848	128,444	140,950	139,345	139,418	135,149
17	141,079	135,385	124,690	133,132	140,894	140,542	138,553	128,251	141,876	139,124	139,069	134,841
18	141,653	134,859	124,326	133,258	140,838	140,338	138,461	128,005	141,746	143,107	138,737	134,444
19	141,468	134,498	123,911	133,348	140,894	140,338	138,223	127,794	141,245	145,152	138,903	134,102
20	141,208	134,318	123,531	133,401	140,913	140,282	137,948	127,548	140,820	143,219	139,308	133,743
21	140,894	134,049	123,101	133,653	140,857	140,116	137,637	127,320	140,727	142,323	139,381	133,437
22	140,727	133,851	122,756	133,905	140,616	139,988	137,273	127,059	140,913	141,857	139,363	133,114
23	140,616	133,599	122,498	133,959	140,634	139,859	137,017	126,743	140,801	141,542	139,179	132,755
24	140,894	133,186	121,985	134,049	140,597	139,730	136,672	126,796	140,690	140,913	138,958	132,415
25	143,480	132,880	121,608	133,959	140,486	139,767	136,236	126,883	140,505	140,468	138,756	132,200
26	142,789	132,558	121,197	133,995	140,634	139,840	135,910	126,831	140,338	140,431	138,958	132,433
27	142,304	132,272	120,821	134,300	140,950	140,301	135,602	126,866	140,043	140,356	139,161	132,486
28	141,931	132,004	120,395	135,222	141,153	140,616	135,149	128,602	140,043	140,135	139,400	132,612
29	141,709	131,719	120,004	136,073	141,282	140,672	134,714	129,678	140,080	141,153	139,271	134,516
30	141,542	131,487		136,690	141,282	140,616	134,264	130,387	140,043	141,171	138,995	135,964
31	141,412	131,007		137,163		140,505		130,883	139,785		138,701	
Change	-650	-10,405	-11,003	+17,159	+4,119	-777	-6,241	-3,381	+8,902	+1,386	-2,470	-2,737
Equiv. Mgal/d	-21.0	-335.6	-379.4	+553.5	+137.3	-25.1	-208.0	-109.1	+287.2	+46.2	-79.7	-91.2
Equiv. ft³/s	-32.4	-519	-587	+856	+212	-38.8	-322	-169	+444	+71.5	-123	-141

Change for year -6,098 Mgal   Equivalent for year -16.7 Mgal/d   Equivalent for year -25.8 ft³/s

23

Table 4. Storage in Cannonsville Reservoir, New York, for year ending November 30, 2004.
(River Master daily operations record; gage reading at 0800 hours)

[Storage in millions of gallons above elevation 1,040.00 ft.   Add 2,584 million gallons for total contents above sill outlet tunnel, elevation 1,020.50 ft. Storage at spillway level is 95,706 million gallons]

DAY	DEC	JAN	FEB	MAR	APR	MAY	JUNE	JULY	AUG	SEPT	OCT	NOV
1	98,088	98,297	94,870	88,998	98,104	97,524	97,041	89,743	87,349	95,311	96,109	96,961
2	98,056	98,120	94,671	88,861	98,088	97,428	97,057	89,256	88,042	95,311	95,948	96,735
3	98,007	97,975	94,489	89,165	98,088	97,685	97,057	88,541	88,571	95,296	95,899	96,559
4	97,959	98,136	94,337	90,306	97,975	97,959	97,138	87,811	88,952	95,235	95,770	96,398
5	97,911	98,474	94,155	91,736	97,798	97,862	97,073	87,103	89,180	95,220	95,630	96,318
6	97,750	98,555	94,018	94,170	97,653	97,846	97,009	86,597	89,484	95,189	95,554	96,286
7	97,605	98,458	93,927	98,249	97,540	97,798	96,945	86,019	89,682	95,144	95,448	96,237
8	97,508	98,265	93,911	99,585	97,460	97,685	96,671	85,658	89,682	95,144	95,432	96,092
9	97,363	98,104	93,820	99,456	97,347	97,540	96,237	85,268	89,606	95,630	95,706	95,819
10	97,235	97,782	93,699	99,070	97,267	97,444	95,948	84,646	89,423	96,044	96,028	95,417
11	97,267	97,540	93,592	98,619	97,170	97,524	95,770	84,097	89,271	95,819	96,253	95,615
12	99,392	97,476	93,501	98,233	97,041	97,460	95,554	83,678	89,165	95,569	96,382	95,964
13	99,650	97,508	93,379	98,120	97,057	97,524	95,311	83,330	89,591	95,508	96,414	96,205
14	99,215	97,492	93,135	97,814	97,492	97,444	95,113	83,013	90,488	95,402	96,479	96,382
15	98,893	97,363	92,862	97,718	97,701	97,347	94,931	82,897	91,066	95,356	96,543	96,495
16	98,716	96,977	92,618	97,557	97,718	97,315	94,702	82,782	91,705	95,326	96,816	96,511
17	98,233	96,607	92,299	97,476	97,653	97,267	94,489	82,565	92,634	95,296	96,832	96,575
18	98,394	96,447	92,025	97,363	97,589	96,880	94,231	82,333	93,379	98,200	96,880	96,591
19	98,490	96,334	91,751	97,251	97,573	96,687	93,866	82,102	93,896	104,145	96,961	96,623
20	98,281	96,189	91,431	97,138	97,573	96,511	93,547	81,987	94,383	102,530	97,267	96,655
21	98,088	96,092	91,066	97,122	97,508	96,479	93,242	81,669	94,641	100,888	97,154	96,671
22	97,846	96,028	90,716	97,315	97,412	96,431	92,922	81,163	95,387	99,874	97,202	96,703
23	97,734	95,915	90,580	97,235	97,299	96,398	92,634	80,696	95,600	99,086	97,235	96,703
24	97,862	95,867	90,275	97,186	97,299	96,302	92,314	80,640	95,786	98,152	97,251	96,687
25	100,598	95,738	89,986	97,202	97,251	96,302	91,964	80,627	95,691	97,186	97,235	96,752
26	101,162	95,615	89,743	97,315	97,251	96,189	91,645	80,557	95,584	96,559	97,202	97,251
27	100,502	95,493	89,560	97,589	97,621	96,157	91,324	80,571	95,539	95,980	97,170	97,508
28	99,810	95,417	89,332	98,136	97,685	97,331	91,051	82,767	95,493	95,931	97,138	97,685
29	99,231	95,296	89,059	98,410	97,669	97,444	90,701	84,718	95,356	96,800	97,073	99,424
30	98,683	95,220		98,410	97,605	97,331	90,168	85,846	95,128	96,431	97,025	99,521
31	98,555	95,007		98,265		97,154		86,641	95,220		96,977	
Change	+161	-3,548	-5,948	+9,206	-660	-451	-6,986	-3,527	+8,579	+1,211	+546	+2,544
Equiv. Mgal/d	+5.2	-114.5	-205.1	+297.0	-22.0	-14.5	-232.9	-113.8	+276.7	+40.4	+17.6	+84.8
Equiv. ft³/s	+8.0	-177	-317	+459	-34.0	-22.5	-360	-176	+428	+62.4	+27.2	+131

Change for year +1,127 Mgal   Equivalent for year +3.1 Mgal/d   Equivalent for year +4.8 ft³/s

24

Table 5. Storage in Neversink Reservoir, New York, for year ending November 30, 2004.
(River Master daily operations record; gage reading at 0800 hours)

[Storage in millions of gallons above elevation 1,319.00 ft. Add 525 million gallons for total contents above sill of outlet tunnel, elevation 1,314.00 ft. Storage at spillway level is 34,941 million gallons]

DAY	DEC	JAN	FEB	MAR	APR	MAY	JUNE	JULY	AUG	SEPT	OCT	NOV
1	34,729	34,749	35,036	35,001	32,671	33,979	34,586	33,221	34,808	34,419	34,769	32,481
2	35,006	34,926	35,046	35,031	33,110	33,949	34,675	33,077	34,665	34,277	34,655	32,548
3	35,115	35,080	35,041	35,066	33,408	33,983	34,808	32,967	34,502	34,130	34,527	32,634
4	35,130	35,155	35,056	35,046	33,577	34,033	34,744	32,848	34,326	33,896	34,374	32,643
5	35,135	35,229	35,016	34,808	33,717	34,028	34,670	32,723	34,121	33,717	34,547	32,567
6	35,135	35,189	35,031	34,562	33,794	34,023	34,645	32,624	34,042	33,533	34,670	32,325
7	35,135	35,155	35,056	34,680	33,939	34,165	34,562	32,514	33,944	33,331	34,833	32,052
8	35,130	35,140	35,046	34,675	33,949	34,160	34,562	32,430	33,746	33,144	34,966	31,790
9	35,150	35,140	35,041	34,482	33,949	34,160	34,532	32,321	33,543	33,197	34,818	31,818
10	35,150	35,100	35,041	34,209	33,964	34,145	34,552	32,175	33,317	33,857	34,562	31,888
11	35,140	35,085	35,041	33,915	33,983	34,199	34,562	32,052	33,081	34,028	34,306	31,962
12	35,428	35,120	35,036	33,606	34,033	34,228	34,581	31,906	33,125	33,959	34,394	32,014
13	35,244	35,135	35,041	33,307	34,091	34,184	34,620	31,804	34,326	33,833	34,468	31,846
14	35,184	35,061	35,036	32,976	34,355	34,224	34,630	31,677	35,254	33,693	34,482	31,527
15	35,174	35,056	35,026	32,634	34,277	34,238	34,635	31,686	35,194	33,499	34,370	31,266
16	35,140	35,051	35,011	32,292	34,126	34,243	34,502	31,667	35,165	33,432	34,086	30,966
17	35,145	35,051	34,991	32,227	34,086	34,209	34,350	31,583	35,174	33,374	33,842	30,818
18	35,189	35,056	34,996	32,170	34,052	34,194	34,306	31,513	35,110	34,404	33,591	30,625
19	35,155	35,061	34,996	32,118	34,008	34,219	34,316	31,466	35,051	35,409	33,703	30,406
20	35,135	35,051	35,001	32,052	33,988	34,189	34,263	31,405	35,046	35,204	33,974	30,191
21	35,120	35,051	35,001	32,028	33,935	34,199	34,199	31,275	34,931	35,150	34,111	29,950
22	35,115	35,051	34,996	31,991	33,823	34,228	34,219	31,076	35,031	34,981	34,003	29,706
23	35,120	35,031	34,991	31,906	33,727	34,233	34,101	30,937	34,946	34,892	33,751	29,455
24	35,150	35,031	34,986	31,822	33,803	34,277	33,959	33,048	34,808	34,719	33,489	29,204
25	35,538	35,031	35,001	31,728	33,818	34,389	33,872	33,577	34,685	34,502	33,245	29,096
26	35,284	35,036	35,006	31,677	33,954	34,404	33,770	33,823	34,522	34,277	33,341	29,114
27	35,204	35,036	35,006	31,761	34,394	34,665	33,703	34,047	34,360	34,033	33,432	28,981
28	35,179	35,051	35,006	32,056	34,365	34,695	33,591	34,537	34,189	33,852	33,485	28,861
29	35,174	35,041	35,001	32,278	34,209	34,749	33,475	34,897	34,180	34,606	33,360	30,378
30	35,011	35,036		32,401	34,023	34,675	33,350	34,961	34,033	34,778	33,057	30,850
31	34,853	35,036		32,524		34,625		34,887	34,350		32,752	
Change	+129	+183	-35	-2,477	+1,499	+602	-1,275	+1,537	-537	+428	-2,026	-1,902
Equiv. Mgal/d	+4.2	+5.9	-1.2	-79.9	+50.0	+19.4	-42.5	+49.6	-17.3	+14.3	-65.4	-63.4
Equiv. ft³/s	+6.4	+9.1	-1.9	-124	+77.3	+30.0	-65.7	+76.7	-26.8	+22.1	-101	-98.1

Change for year -3,874 Mgal   Equivalent for year -10.6 Mgal/d   Equivalent for year -16.4 ft³/s

Table 6. Design rates for Delaware River at Montague, New Jersey, gaging station, December 1, 2003, to November 30, 2004.

[Rates in cubic feet per second]

Effective dates	Montague Design Rate
December 1, 2003, to March 14, 2004	1,810
March 15 to June 14, 2004	1,750
June 15 to November 30, 2004	1,820

Table 7. Consumption of water by New York City, 1950 to 2004.
(Data furnished by New York City, Department of Environmental Protection, Bureau of Water Supply)

[Mgal/d, million gallons per day; Bgal, billion gallons]

| Year | Average daily consumption | | | Annual Consumption (Bgal) |
	City Proper (Mgal/d)	Outside Communities (Mgal/d)	Total (Mgal/d)	
1950	953.3	29.1	982.4	358.576
51	1,041.9	28.1	1,070.0	390.550
52	1,087.0	32.7	1,119.7	409.810
53	1,093.9	44.6	1,138.5	415.552
54	1,063.4	46.3	1,109.7	405.040
1955	1,109.9	45.3	1,155.2	421.648
56	1,111.3	48.9	1,160.2	424.633
57	1,169.0	57.2	1,226.2	447.563
58	1,152.9	49.6	1,202.5	438.912
59	1,204.3	60.3	1,264.6	461.579
1960	1,199.4	58.9	1,258.3	460.529
61	1,221.0	64.0	1,285.0	469.022
62	1,207.6	68.8	1,276.4	465.896
63	1,218.0	76.7	1,294.7	472.582
64	1,189.2	79.4	1,268.6	464.295
1965	1,052.1	71.2	1,123.3	409.995
66	1,044.9	73.2	1,118.1	408.128
67	1,135.3	71.0	1,206.3	440.302
68	1,242.0	78.2	1,320.2	483.175
69	1,328.7	80.1	1,408.8	514.229
1970	1,400.3	90.4	1,490.7	544.116
71	1,423.6	87.9	1,511.5	551.695
72	1,412.4	83.0	1,495.4	547.340
73	1,448.9	95.4	1,544.3	563.681
74	1,441.8	96.3	1,538.1	561.409
1975	1,415.0	92.1	1,507.1	550.093
76	1,435.0	95.8	1,530.8	560.264
77	1,483.0	104.7	1,587.7	579.510
78	1,479.4	103.0	1,582.4	577.566
79	1,513.0	104.6	1,617.6	590.426
1980	1,506.3	110.1	1,616.3	591.582
81	1,309.5	100.0	1,409.5	514.475
82	1,383.0	104.8	1,487.8	543.060
83	1,424.2	112.6	1,536.8	561.010
84	1,465.2	113.9	1,579.1	577.963
1985	1,325.4	106.5	1,431.9	522.656
86	1,351.1	115.2	1,466.3	535.200
87	1,447.1	119.8	1,566.9	571.885
88	1,484.3	125.6	1,609.9	589.090
89	1,402.0	113.4	1,515.4	553.158
1990	1,424.4	122.4	1,546.8	564.577
91	1,469.9	123.6	1,593.5	581.628
92	1,368.7	113.9	1,482.6	542.632
93	1,368.9	118.8	1,487.7	543.011
94	1,357.8	119.2	1,477.0	539.105
1995	1,326.1	123.1	1,449.2	528.958
96	1,283.5	120.2	1,403.7	512.351
97	1,201.3	123.5	1,324.8	483.552
98	1,220.0	124.7	1,344.7	490.816
99	1,237.2	128.6	1,365.8	498.517
2000	1,240.4	124.9	1,365.3	499.700
01	1,184.0	128.4	1,312.4	479.026
02	1,135.6	121.1	1,256.7	458.696
03	1,093.7	115.9	1,209.6	441.516
04	1,099.6	117.5	1,217.1	445.461

Table 8. New York City reservoir release design data.—Continued.
(River Master daily operation record)

[ft3/s, cubic feet per second; (ft³/s)-d, cubic feet per second days; Col., Column]

Date of advance estimate	Powerplant release forecasts — Lake Wallenpaupack (ft³/s) Col. 1	Rio Reservoir (ft³/s) Col. 2	Uncontrolled runoff — Current condition (ft³/s) Col. 3	Weather adjustment (ft³/s) Col. 4	Montague date 2004	Discharge (ft³/s) Col. 5	Indicated deficiency Col. 6	Balancing adjustment (ft³/s) Col. 7	Directed release (ft³/s) Col. 8	Adjusted directed release Daily (ft³/s) Col. 9	Cumulative (ft³/s)-d Col. 10	Actual deficiency Daily (ft³/s) Col. 11	Cumulative (ft³/s)-d Col. 12	Cumulative difference (ft³/s)-d Col. 13	Balancing adjustment (ft³/s) Col. 14
June 14	378	0	1,281	47	June 17	1,706	114	--	114	114	114	0	0	114	-11
15	378	0	1,250	21	18	1,649	171	--	171	171	285	0	0	285	-28
16	378	0	1,200	38	19	1,616	204	0	204	204	489	0	0	489	-49
17	0	0	1,108	95	20	1,203	617	0	617	623	1,112	113	113	999	-70
18	0	0	1,817	1	21	1,818	2	-11	0	0	1,112	403	516	596	-60
19	359	0	1,408	25	22	1,792	28	-28	0	0	1,112	236	752	360	-36
20	359	0	1,287	50	23	1,696	124	-49	75	75	1,187	329	1,081	106	-11
21	359	0	1,210	37	24	1,606	214	-70	144	144	1,331	373	1,454	-123	+12
22	359	0	1,074	22	25	1,455	365	-60	305	305	1,636	421	1,875	-239	+24
23	359	0	1,158	3	26	1,520	300	-36	264	264	1,900	514	2,389	-489	+49
24	0	142	1,091	200	27	1,433	387	-11	376	376	2,276	487	2,876	-600	+60
25	0	0	908	324	28	1,232	588	+12	600	600	2,876	487	3,363	-487	+49
26	288	0	1,210	21	29	1,519	301	+24	325	325	3,201	436	3,799	-598	+60
27	288	0	1,154	47	30	1,489	331	+49	380	380	3,581	534	4,333	-752	+70

MONTAGUE DESIGN RATE = 1,810 (ft³/s) DECEMBER 1, 2003, to MARCH 14, 2004
The estimated Montague discharge was greater than the Montague design rate from December 1, 2003, to March 15, 2004

MONTAGUE DESIGN RATE = 1,750 (ft³/s) MARCH 15, 2004, to JUNE 14, 2004
The estimated Montague discharge was greater than the Montague design rate March 16, 2004, to June 14, 2004

MONTAGUE DESIGN RATE = 1,820 (ft³/s) JUNE 15, 2004, to NOVEMBER 30, 2004
The estimated Montague discharge was greater than the Montague design rate June 15 and 16, 2004

Col. 1 - Furnished by power company.
Col. 2 - Furnished by power company.
Col. 3 - Computed from index stations.
Col. 4 - Computed increase in runoff based on quantitative precipitation forecasts.
Col. 5 = Col. 1 + Col. 2 + Col. 3 + Col. 4.

Col. 6 = Design rate - Col. 5, when positive; otherwise Col. 6 = 0.
Col. 7 = Col. 14 (4 days earlier).
Col. 8 = Design rate - Col. 5 + Col. 7, when positive; otherwise Col. 8 = 0.
Col. 9 = Col. 7 from Table 9.
Col. 10 = Summation of Col. 9.

Col. 11 = Design rate - (Col. 9 + Col. 10 from Table 9), when positive; otherwise Col. 11 = 0.
Col. 12 = Summation of Col. 11.
Col. 13 = Col. 10 - Col. 12.
Col. 14 = Col. 13 divided by -10, limited to ±70.

Table 8. New York City reservoir release design data—Continued.
(River Master daily operation record)

[ft3/s, cubic feet per second; (ft³/s)-d, cubic feet per second days; Col., Column]

| Date of advance estimate | Powerplant release forecasts | | Uncontrolled runoff | | Montague date | Discharge | Indicated deficiency | Balancing adjustment | Directed release | Adjusted directed release | | Actual deficiency | | Cumulative difference | Balancing adjustment |
| | Lake Wallenpaupack (ft³/s) | Rio Reservoir (ft³/s) | Current condition (ft³/s) | Weather adjustment (ft³/s) | | (ft³/s) | (ft³/s) | (ft³/s) | (ft³/s) | Daily (ft³/s) | Cumulative (ft³/s)-d | Daily (ft³/s) | Cumulative (ft³/s)-d | (ft³/s)-d | (ft³/s) |
2004	Col. 1	Col. 2	Col. 3	Col. 4	2004	Col. 5	Col. 6	Col. 7	Col. 8	Col. 9	Col. 10	Col. 11	Col. 12	Col. 13	Col. 14
June 28	288	0	840	9	July 1	1,137	683	+60	743	739	4,320	719	5,052	-732	+70
29	288	0	991	7	2	1,286	534	+49	583	586	4,906	696	5,748	-842	+70
30	288	0	944	19	3	1,251	569	+60	629	641	5,547	871	6,619	-1,072	+70
July 1	0	0	869	19	4	888	932	+70	1,002	1,002	6,549	1,122	7,741	-1,192	+70
2	0	0	848	12	5	860	960	+70	1,030	1,029	7,578	1,109	8,850	-1,272	+70
3	0	0	772	11	6	783	1,037	+70	1,107	1,108	8,686	1,138	9,988	-1,302	+70
4	311	0	670	6	7	987	833	+70	903	904	9,590	574	10,562	-972	+70
5	311	0	656	3	8	970	850	+70	920	919	10,509	409	10,971	-462	+46
6	311	0	780	81	9	1,172	648	+70	718	718	11,227	318	11,289	-62	+6
7	311	142	808	85	10	1,346	474	+70	544	544	11,771	334	11,623	148	-15
8	0	0	807	9	11	816	1,004	+70	1,074	1,074	12,845	1,024	12,647	198	-20
9	0	0	857	0	12	857	963	+46	1,009	990	13,835	1,070	13,717	118	-12
10	311	0	769	3	13	1,083	737	+6	743	743	14,578	553	14,270	308	-31
11	335	0	719	86	14	1,140	680	-15	665	667	15,245	317	14,587	658	-66
12	311	0	671	419	15	1,401	419	-20	399	399	15,644	10	14,597	1,047	-70
13	311	0	814	313	16	1,438	382	-12	370	370	16,014	0	14,597	1,417	-70
14	423	0	886	122	17	1,431	389	-31	358	358	16,372	0	14,597	1,775	-70
15	0	0	1,782	6	18	1,788	32	-66	0	0	16,372	0	14,597	1,775	-70
16	0	0	1,783	26	19	1,809	11	-70	0	0	16,372	0	14,597	1,775	-70
Aug. 10	382	0	1,256	42	Aug. 13	1,680	140	-70	70	70	16,442	0	14,597	1,845	-70

MONTAGUE DESIGN RATE = 1,750 (ft³/s) May 29, 2002, to November 30, 2002

The estimated discharge at Montague was greater than the Montague design rate from May 29, 2002, to July 6, 2002.

The estimated Montague discharge was greater than the Montague design rate from July 20, 2004, to August 12, 2004.

The estimated Montague discharge was greater than the Montague design rate from August 14, 2004, to November 30, 2004.

Col. 1 - Furnished by power company.
Col. 2 - Furnished by power company.
Col. 3 - Computed from index stations.
Col. 4 - Computed increase in runoff based on quantitative precipitation forecasts.
Col. 5 = Col. 1 + Col. 2 + Col. 3 + Col. 4.

Col. 6 = Design rate - Col. 5, when positive; otherwise Col. 6 = 0.
Col. 7 = Col. 14 (4 days earlier).
Col. 8 = Design rate - Col. 5 + Col. 7, when positive; otherwise Col. 8 = 0.
Col. 9 = Col. 7 from Table 9.
Col. 10 = Summation of Col. 9.

Col. 11 = Design rate - (Col. 9 + Col. 10 from Table 9), when positive; otherwise Col. 11 = 0.
Col. 12 = Summation of Col. 11.
Col. 13 = Col. 10 - Col. 12.
Col. 14 = Col. 13 divided by -10, limited to ±70.

Table 9. Controlled releases from reservoirs in the upper Delaware River Basin and segregation of flow of Delaware River at Montague, New Jersey. (River Master daily operation record)

[Mean discharge in cubic feet per second for 24 hours; Col., Column; Cumul., Cumulative]

Controlled Releases from New York City Reservoirs					Controlled Releases from Power Reservoirs			Segregation of Flow, Delaware River at Montague, New Jersey							
	Directed								Controlled Releases					Excess Release Credits	
									New York City Reservoirs		Power-plants	Computed uncon-trolled	Total		
Date	Amount	Pepac-ton	Cannons-ville	Never-sink	Date	Lake Wallenpau-pack	Rio Reservoir	Date	Directed	Other				Daily	Cumul.
2003	Col. 1	Col. 2	Col. 3	Col. 4	2003	Col. 5	Col. 6	2003	Col. 7	Col. 8	Col. 9	Col. 10	Col. 11	Col. 12	Col. 13
Nov. 28	0	45	46	25	Nov. 30	537	738	Dec. 1	0	116	1,275	14,609	16,000	0	2,994
29	0	45	46	25	Dec. 1	594	762	2	0	116	1,356	12,228	13,700	0	2,994
30	0	45	46	25	2	819	851	3	0	116	1,670	10,214	12,000	0	2,994
Dec. 1	0	45	46	25	3	816	794	4	0	116	1,610	9,074	10,800	0	2,994
2	0	45	46	25	4	963	645	5	0	116	1,608	8,206	9,930	0	2,994
3	0	45	46	25	5	924	660	6	0	116	1,584	7,770	9,470	0	2,994
4	0	45	46	25	6	1,002	660	7	0	116	1,662	7,212	8,990	0	2,994
5	0	45	46	25	7	962	450	8	0	116	1,412	6,402	7,930	0	2,994
6	0	45	46	25	8	972	11	9	0	116	983	6,011	7,110	0	2,994
7	0	45	46	25	9	882	142	10	0	116	1,024	5,640	6,780	0	2,994
8	0	45	46	25	10	755	649	11	0	116	1,404	13,680	15,200	0	2,994
9	0	45	46	25	11	1,391	986	12	0	116	2,377	41,107	43,600	0	2,994
10	0	45	46	25	12	1,694	1,245	13	0	116	2,939	26,345	29,400	0	2,994
11	0	45	46	25	13	1,722	1,270	14	0	116	2,992	18,392	21,500	0	2,994
12	0	45	46	25	14	1,722	1,472	15	0	116	3,194	14,990	18,300	0	2,994
13	0	45	46	25	15	1,659	1,255	16	0	116	2,914	12,770	15,800	0	2,994
14	0	45	46	25	16	1,646	1,277	17	0	116	2,923	11,061	14,100	0	2,994
15	0	45	46	25	17	1,702	1,227	18	0	116	2,929	13,355	16,400	0	2,994
16	0	45	46	25	18	1,518	1,184	19	0	116	2,702	12,182	15,000	0	2,994
17	0	45	46	25	19	1,078	918	20	0	116	1,996	10,788	12,900	0	2,994
18	0	45	46	25	20	1,105	766	21	0	116	1,871	9,813	11,800	0	2,994
19	0	594	46	25	21	1,020	482	22	0	665	1,502	8,233	10,400	0	2,994
20	0	713	46	25	22	1,078	355	23	0	784	1,433	7,573	9,790	0	2,994
21	0	713	46	25	23	1,097	599	24	0	784	1,696	11,520	14,000	0	2,994
22	0	713	46	25	24	1,597	706	25	0	784	2,303	35,513	38,600	0	2,994
23	0	661	46	25	25	1,463	730	26	0	732	2,193	28,975	31,900	0	2,994
24	0	45	46	25	26	1,053	770	27	0	116	1,823	22,061	24,000	0	2,994
25	0	45	46	25	27	1,021	752	28	0	116	1,773	17,211	19,100	0	2,994
26	0	45	46	25	28	1,069	791	29	0	116	1,860	13,924	15,900	0	2,994
27	0	45	46	25	29	1,075	816	30	0	116	1,891	11,993	14,000	0	2,994
28	0	45	46	25	30	1,063	734	31	0	116	1,797	11,287	13,200	0	2,994
Total	0	4,564	1,426	775		35,999	24,697		0	6,765	60,696	440,139	507,600		

Col. 2 - 24 hours beginning 1200 of date shown.
Col. 3 - 24 hours ending 2400 one day later.
Col. 4 - 24 hours beginning 1500 one day later.
Col. 5 - 24 hours beginning 0800 of date shown.
Col. 6 - 24 hours beginning 1600 of date shown.

Col. 7 = Col. 2 + Col. 3 + Col. 4 in response to direction (Col. 1).
Col. 8 = Col. 2 + Col. 3 + Col. 4 - Col. 7.
Col. 9 = Col. 5 + Col. 6.
Col. 10 = Col. 11 - Col. 7 - Col. 8 - Col. 9.
Col. 11 = 24 hours of calendar day shown.

Col. 12 = Col. 11 - Col. 8 - 1,750 ft³/s computed arithmetically, but not greater than Col. 7; except that part of Col. 8 contributing to the excess-release increment of Col. 11.

Col. 13 = Summation of Col. 12.

Table 9. Controlled releases from reservoirs in the upper Delaware River Basin and segregation of flow of Delaware River at Montague, New Jersey—Continued. (River Master daily operation record)

[Mean discharge in cubic feet per second for 24 hours; Col., Column; Cumul., Cumulative]

Controlled Releases from New York City Reservoirs					Controlled Releases from Power Reservoirs			Segregation of Flow, Delaware River at Montague, New Jersey							
Directed									Controlled Releases			Computed uncontrolled	Total	Excess Release Credits	
Date	Amount	Pepacton	Cannonsville	Neversink	Date	Lake Wallenpaupack	Rio Reservoir	Date	New York City Reservoirs		Power-plants			Daily	Cumul.
									Directed	Other					
2003/2004	Col. 1	Col. 2	Col. 3	Col. 4	2003/2004	Col. 5	Col. 6	2004	Col. 7	Col. 8	Col. 9	Col. 10	Col. 11	Col. 12	Col. 13
Dec. 29	0	53	46	25	Dec. 31	1,012	727	Jan. 1	0	124	1,739	10,237	12,100	0	2,994
30	0	343	46	25	Jan. 1	1,064	741	2	0	414	1,805	8,881	11,100	0	2,994
31	0	620	46	25	2	1,047	504	3	0	691	1,551	7,958	10,200	0	2,994
Jan. 1	0	709	46	25	3	960	383	4	0	780	1,343	9,277	11,400	0	2,994
2	0	712	46	25	4	1,277	387	5	0	783	1,664	15,653	18,100	0	2,994
3	0	710	46	25	5	1,070	628	6	0	781	1,698	16,521	19,000	0	2,994
4	0	718	46	25	6	996	826	7	0	789	1,822	12,689	15,300	0	2,994
5	0	712	46	25	7	906	762	8	0	783	1,668	10,249	12,700	0	2,994
6	0	710	46	25	8	940	801	9	0	781	1,741	9,378	11,900	0	2,994
7	0	712	46	25	9	1,103	532	10	0	783	1,635	7,562	9,980	0	2,994
8	0	692	46	25	10	1,030	408	11	0	763	1,438	5,969	8,170	0	2,994
9	0	798	46	25	11	913	284	12	0	869	1,197	6,404	8,470	0	2,994
10	0	801	46	25	12	727	521	13	0	872	1,248	6,570	8,690	0	2,994
11	0	800	46	25	13	788	677	14	0	871	1,465	5,924	8,260	0	2,994
12	0	806	46	25	14	515	660	15	0	877	1,175	4,328	6,380	0	2,994
13	0	798	46	25	15	564	670	16	0	869	1,234	3,987	6,090	0	2,994
14	0	798	46	25	16	704	511	17	0	869	1,215	4,396	6,480	0	2,994
15	0	797	46	25	17	872	422	18	0	868	1,294	5,048	7,210	0	2,994
16	0	794	46	25	18	878	422	19	0	865	1,300	5,375	7,540	0	2,994
17	0	636	46	25	19	761	479	20	0	707	1,240	4,763	6,710	0	2,994
18	0	246	46	25	20	696	181	21	0	317	877	4,346	5,540	0	2,994
19	0	45	46	25	21	735	209	22	0	116	944	3,990	5,050	0	2,994
20	0	45	46	25	22	705	213	23	0	116	918	3,706	4,740	0	2,994
21	0	45	46	25	23	742	191	24	0	116	933	3,731	4,780	0	2,994
22	0	45	46	25	24	830	188	25	0	116	1,018	3,336	4,470	0	2,994
23	0	45	46	25	25	696	124	26	0	116	820	3,264	4,200	0	2,994
24	0	45	46	25	26	552	135	27	0	116	687	3,297	4,100	0	2,994
25	0	45	46	25	27	597	174	28	0	116	771	3,113	4,000	0	2,994
26	0	45	46	25	28	563	181	29	0	116	744	3,140	4,000	0	2,994
27	0	45	71	25	29	518	206	30	0	141	724	2,935	3,800	0	2,994
28	0	45	88	25	30	493	149	31	0	158	642	3,000	3,800	0	2,994
Total	0	14,415	1,493	775		25,254	13,296		0	16,683	38,550	199,027	254,260		

Col. 2 - 24 hours beginning 1200 of date shown.
Col. 3 - 24 hours ending 2400 one day later.
Col. 4 - 24 hours beginning 1500 one day later.
Col. 5 - 24 hours beginning 0800 of date shown.
Col. 6 - 24 hours beginning 1600 of date shown.

Col. 7 = Col. 2 + Col. 3 + Col. 4 in response to direction (Col. 1).
Col. 8 = Col. 2 + Col. 3 + Col. 4 - Col. 7.
Col. 9 = Col. 5 + Col. 6.
Col. 10 = Col. 11 - Col. 7 - Col. 8 - Col. 9.
Col. 11 = 24 hours of calendar day shown.

Col. 12 = Col. 11 - Col. 8 - 1,750 ft³/s computed arithmetically, but not greater than Col. 7; except that part of Col. 8 contributing to the excess-release increment of Col. 11.

Col. 13 = Summation of Col. 12.

31

Table 9. Controlled releases from reservoirs in the upper Delaware River Basin and segregation of flow of Delaware River at Montague, New Jersey—Continued. (River Master daily operation record)

[Mean discharge in cubic feet per second for 24 hours; Col., Column; Cumul., Cumulative]

Controlled Releases from New York City Reservoirs					Controlled Releases from Power Reservoirs			Segregation of Flow, Delaware River at Montague, New Jersey							
Directed		Pepacton	Cannonsville	Neversink	Date	Lake Wallenpaupack	Rio Reservoir	Date	Controlled Releases			Computed uncontrolled	Total	Excess Release Credits	
Date 2004	Amount				2004			2004	New York City Reservoirs		Power-plants			Daily	Cumul.
									Directed	Other					
	Col. 1	Col. 2	Col. 3	Col. 4		Col. 5	Col. 6		Col. 7	Col. 8	Col. 9	Col. 10	Col. 11	Col. 12	Col. 13
Jan. 29	0	45	73	25	Jan. 31	0	106	Feb. 1	0	143	106	2,951	3,200	0	2,994
30	0	45	87	25	Feb. 1	131	89	2	0	157	220	2,623	3,000	0	2,994
31	0	45	85	25	2	300	124	3	0	155	424	2,921	3,500	0	2,994
Feb. 1	0	45	96	25	3	363	124	4	0	166	487	2,747	3,400	0	2,994
2	0	45	88	25	4	346	113	5	0	158	459	2,683	3,300	0	2,994
3	0	45	96	25	5	310	117	6	0	166	427	2,607	3,200	0	2,994
4	0	53	87	25	6	292	160	7	0	165	452	2,583	3,200	0	2,994
5	0	85	102	25	7	0	160	8	0	212	160	2,728	3,100	0	2,994
6	0	45	130	25	8	70	160	9	0	200	230	2,670	3,100	0	2,994
7	0	45	122	25	9	365	152	10	0	192	517	2,691	3,400	0	2,994
8	0	45	119	25	10	434	163	11	0	189	597	2,414	3,200	0	2,994
9	0	45	127	25	11	353	170	12	0	197	523	2,380	3,100	0	2,994
10	0	45	139	25	12	331	191	13	0	209	522	2,269	3,000	0	2,994
11	0	45	141	25	13	268	195	14	0	211	463	2,226	2,900	0	2,994
12	0	45	139	25	14	0	177	15	0	209	177	2,114	2,500	0	2,994
13	0	45	142	25	15	51	174	16	0	212	225	2,063	2,500	0	2,994
14	0	45	152	25	16	315	156	17	0	222	471	2,207	2,900	0	2,994
15	0	45	159	25	17	369	145	18	0	229	514	1,957	2,700	0	2,994
16	0	45	164	25	18	282	85	19	0	234	367	1,999	2,600	0	2,994
17	0	45	169	25	19	355	89	20	0	239	444	1,917	2,600	0	2,994
18	0	45	173	25	20	317	89	21	0	243	406	1,951	2,600	0	2,994
19	0	45	176	25	21	0	0	22	0	246	0	1,954	2,200	0	2,994
20	0	45	204	25	22	0	0	23	0	274	0	1,956	2,230	0	2,994
21	0	43	229	25	23	106	103	24	0	297	209	1,984	2,490	0	2,994
22	0	45	189	25	24	82	71	25	0	259	153	1,998	2,410	0	2,994
23	0	43	149	25	25	70	71	26	0	217	141	1,832	2,190	0	2,994
24	0	43	144	25	26	105	71	27	0	212	176	1,752	2,140	0	2,994
25	0	43	158	25	27	64	53	28	0	226	117	1,717	2,060	0	2,994
26	0	43	166	25	28	0	0	29	0	234	0	1,636	1,870	60	3,054
Total	0	1,343	4,005	725		5,679	3,308		0	6,073	8,987	65,530	80,590	60	

Col. 2 - 24 hours beginning 1200 of date shown.
Col. 3 - 24 hours ending 2400 one day later.
Col. 4 - 24 hours beginning 1500 one day later.
Col. 5 - 24 hours beginning 0800 of date shown.
Col. 6 - 24 hours beginning 1600 of date shown.

Col. 7 = Col. 2 + Col. 3 + Col. 4 in response to direction (Col. 1).
Col. 8 = Col. 2 + Col. 3 + Col. 4 - Col. 7.
Col. 9 = Col. 5 + Col. 6.
Col. 10 = Col. 11 - Col. 7 - Col. 8 - Col. 9.
Col. 11 = 24 hours of calendar day shown.

Col. 12 = Col. 8 - 1,750 ft³/s computed arithmetically, but not greater than Col. 7; except that part of Col. 8 contributing to the excess-release increment of Col. 11.

Col. 13 = Summation of Col. 12.

Table 9. Controlled releases from reservoirs in the upper Delaware River Basin and segregation of flow of Delaware River at Montague, New Jersey—Continued.
(River Master daily operation record)

[Mean discharge in cubic feet per second for 24 hours; Col., Column; Cumul., Cumulative]

Controlled Releases from New York City Reservoirs					Controlled Releases from Power Reservoirs			Segregation of Flow, Delaware River at Montague, New Jersey								
Directed		Pepac-ton	Cannons-ville	Never-sink	Date	Lake Wallenpaupack	Rio Reservoir	Controlled Releases			Computed uncon-trolled	Total	Excess Release Credits		Date	
Date 2004	Amount				2004			New York City Reservoirs		Power-plants			Daily	Cumul.	2004	
								Directed	Other							
	Col. 1	Col. 2	Col. 3	Col. 4		Col. 5	Col. 6	Col. 7	Col. 8	Col. 9	Col. 10	Col. 11	Col. 12	Col. 13		
Feb. 27	0	45	170	25	Feb. 29	0	0	0	240	0	1,760	2,000	50	3,104	Mar. 1	
28	0	45	181	25	Mar. 1	100	0	0	251	100	2,179	2,530	0	3,104	2	
29	0	45	183	25	2	128	0	0	253	128	3,959	4,340	0	3,104	3	
Mar. 1	0	45	167	25	3	75	0	0	237	75	7,438	7,750	0	3,104	4	
2	0	45	116	25	4	95	14	0	186	109	9,905	10,200	0	3,104	5	
3	0	45	60	25	5	172	74	0	130	246	11,824	12,200	0	3,104	6	
4	0	45	45	25	6	0	89	0	115	89	19,196	19,400	0	3,104	7	
5	0	45	45	25	7	27	124	0	115	151	17,134	17,400	0	3,104	8	
6	0	46	45	25	8	399	142	0	116	541	13,943	14,600	0	3,104	9	
7	0	46	45	25	9	364	124	0	116	488	11,696	12,300	0	3,104	10	
8	0	46	45	25	10	340	184	0	116	524	10,060	10,700	0	3,104	11	
9	0	46	45	25	11	373	163	0	116	536	9,148	9,800	0	3,104	12	
10	0	46	45	25	12	268	167	0	116	435	8,149	8,700	0	3,104	13	
11	0	45	45	25	13	46	177	0	115	223	7,072	7,410	0	3,104	14	
12	0	45	45	25	14	8	167	0	115	175	6,590	6,880	0	3,104	15	
13	0	278	45	25	15	309	188	0	348	497	6,355	7,200			16	
14	0	761	45	25	16	313	319	0	831	632	5,097	6,560			17	
15	0	138	45	25	17	263	316	0	208	579	5,303	6,090			18	
16	0	45	45	25	18	265	351	0	115	616	5,019	5,750			19	
17	0	45	45	25	19	267	351	0	115	618	4,647	5,380			20	
18	0	45	45	25	20	0	362	0	115	362	4,803	5,280			21	
19	0	45	45	25	21	27	177	0	115	204	5,851	6,170			22	
20	0	45	45	25	22	414	319	0	115	733	5,062	5,910			23	
21	0	45	45	25	23	437	227	0	115	664	4,591	5,370			24	
22	0	45	45	25	24	358	252	0	115	610	4,985	5,710			25	
23	0	45	45	25	25	677	234	0	115	911	5,154	6,180			26	
24	0	45	45	25	26	343	230	0	115	573	5,772	6,460			27	
25	0	45	45	25	27	0	230	0	115	230	7,935	8,280			28	
26	0	45	45	25	28	8	71	0	115	79	8,686	8,880			29	
27	0	45	45	25	29	331	245	0	115	576	7,839	8,530			30	
28	0	45	45	25	30	402	235	0	115	637	7,398	8,150			31	
Total	0	2,442	2,002	775		6,809	5,532	0	5,219	12,341	234,550	252,110				

Col. 2 - 24 hours beginning 1200 of date shown.
Col. 3 - 24 hours ending 2400 one day later.
Col. 4 - 24 hours beginning 1500 one day later.
Col. 5 - 24 hours beginning 0800 of date shown.
Col. 6 - 24 hours beginning 1600 of date shown.

Col. 7 = Col. 2 + Col. 3 + Col. 4 in response to direction (Col. 1).
Col. 8 = Col. 2 + Col. 3 + Col. 4 - Col. 7.
Col. 9 = Col. 5 + Col. 6.
Col. 10 = Col. 11 - Col. 7 - Col. 8 - Col. 9.
Col. 11 = 24 hours of calendar day shown.

Col. 12 = Col. 11 - Col. 8 - 1,750 ft^3/s computed arithmetically, but not greater than Col. 7; except that part of Col. 8 contributing to the excess-release increment of Col. 11.

Col. 13 = Summation of Col. 12.

Table 9. Controlled releases from reservoirs in the upper Delaware River Basin and segregation of flow of Delaware River at Montague, New Jersey—Continued. (River Master daily operation record)

[Mean discharge in cubic feet per second for 24 hours; Col., Column; Cumul., Cumulative]

Controlled Releases from New York City Reservoirs					Controlled Releases from Power Reservoirs			Segregation of Flow, Delaware River at Montague, New Jersey					
Directed		Pepacton	Cannons-ville	Never-sink		Lake Wallenpaupack	Rio Reservoir		Controlled Releases			Computed uncon-trolled	Total
Date	Amount				Date			Date	New York City Reservoirs		Power-plants		
2004					2004			2004	Directed	Other			
	Col. 1	Col. 2	Col. 3	Col. 4		Col. 5	Col. 6		Col. 7	Col. 8	Col. 9	Col. 10	Col. 11
Mar. 29	0	45	45	25	Mar. 31	242	230	Apr. 1	0	115	472	7,593	8,180
30	0	45	45	25	Apr. 1	385	248	2	0	115	633	9,252	10,000
31	0	45	45	25	2	275	206	3	0	115	481	9,014	9,610
Apr. 1	0	45	45	25	3	0	379	4	0	115	379	7,926	8,420
2	0	45	45	25	4	98	383	5	0	115	481	7,474	8,070
3	0	43	42	25	5	1,004	284	6	0	110	1,288	6,342	7,740
4	0	45	45	25	6	1,018	376	7	0	115	1,394	5,361	6,870
5	0	45	45	25	7	424	255	8	0	115	679	5,386	6,180
6	0	45	45	25	8	449	230	9	0	115	679	5,276	6,070
7	0	45	45	25	9	455	230	10	0	115	685	4,800	5,600
8	0	45	45	25	10	1	230	11	0	115	231	4,354	4,700
9	0	45	45	25	11	18	0	12	0	115	18	4,067	4,200
10	0	45	45	25	12	339	160	13	0	115	499	4,826	5,440
11	0	45	45	25	13	347	319	14	0	115	666	8,619	9,400
12	0	45	45	25	14	412	298	15	0	115	710	10,275	11,100
13	0	45	45	25	15	355	301	16	0	115	656	8,729	9,500
14	0	45	45	25	16	258	248	17	0	115	506	7,649	8,270
15	0	45	45	25	17	0	71	18	0	115	71	6,854	7,040
16	0	45	45	25	18	0	18	19	0	115	18	6,327	6,460
17	0	45	45	25	19	106	248	20	0	115	354	5,701	6,170
18	0	45	45	25	20	158	294	21	0	115	452	5,293	5,860
19	0	45	45	25	21	191	131	22	0	115	322	5,003	5,440
20	0	45	45	25	22	169	152	23	0	115	321	5,004	5,440
21	0	45	45	25	23	173	177	24	0	115	350	5,955	6,420
22	0	45	45	25	24	0	124	25	0	115	124	5,711	5,950
23	0	45	45	25	25	0	18	26	0	115	18	5,927	6,060
24	0	45	45	25	26	0	301	27	0	115	301	11,184	11,600
25	0	45	45	25	27	0	195	28	0	115	195	10,390	10,700
26	0	45	45	25	28	0	0	29	0	115	0	9,035	9,150
27	0	45	46	25	29	103	103	30	0	116	103	8,051	8,270
Total	0	1,348	1,348	750	Total	6,877	6,209	Total	0	3,446	13,086	207,378	223,910

Col. 2 - 24 hours beginning 1200 of date shown.
Col. 3 - 24 hours ending 2400 one day later.
Col. 4 - 24 hours beginning 1500 one day later.
Col. 5 - 24 hours beginning 0800 of date shown.
Col. 6 - 24 hours beginning 1600 of date shown.

Col. 7 = Col. 2 + Col. 3 + Col. 4 in response to direction (Col. 1).
Col. 8 = Col. 2 + Col. 3 + Col. 4 - Col. 7.
Col. 9 = Col. 5 + Col. 6.
Col. 10 = Col. 11 - Col. 7 - Col. 8 - Col. 9.
Col. 11 = 24 hours of calendar day shown.

Table 9. Controlled releases from reservoirs in the upper Delaware River Basin and segregation of flow of Delaware River at Montague, New Jersey—Continued.

(River Master daily operation record)

[Mean discharge in cubic feet per second for 24 hours; Col., Column; Cumul., Cumulative]

| Controlled Releases from New York City Reservoirs | | | | | Controlled Releases from Power Reservoirs | | | Segregation of Flow, Delaware River at Montague, New Jersey | | | | | |
Date 2004	Directed Amount Col. 1	Pepacton Col. 2	Cannons-ville Col. 3	Never-sink Col. 4	Date 2004	Lake Wallenpaupack Col. 5	Rio Reservoir Col. 6	Date 2004	NYC Reservoirs Directed Col. 7	NYC Reservoirs Other Col. 8	Power-plants Col. 9	Computed uncontrolled Col. 10	Total Col. 11
Apr. 28	0	45	45	25	Apr. 30	0	35	May 1	0	115	35	7,260	7,410
29	0	45	46	25	May 1	0	106	2	0	116	106	6,408	6,630
30	0	45	46	25	2	18	0	3	0	116	18	8,176	8,310
May 1	0	36	46	25	3	445	706	4	0	107	1,151	9,542	10,800
2	0	36	46	25	4	904	0	5	0	107	904	8,149	9,160
3	0	36	46	25	5	984	177	6	0	107	1,161	7,662	8,930
4	0	36	46	25	6	979	230	7	0	107	1,209	7,494	8,810
5	0	36	46	25	7	619	355	8	0	107	974	6,789	7,870
6	0	36	46	25	8	0	142	9	0	107	142	6,541	6,790
7	0	36	46	29	9	81	160	10	0	111	241	6,578	6,930
8	0	43	46	28	10	861	390	11	0	117	1,251	6,582	7,950
9	0	63	46	25	11	983	195	12	0	134	1,178	7,788	9,100
10	0	36	46	25	12	913	496	13	0	107	1,409	8,364	9,880
11	0	36	45	25	13	964	355	14	0	106	1,319	8,295	9,720
12	0	36	60	25	14	754	195	15	0	121	949	7,020	8,090
13	0	36	46	25	15	0	89	16	0	107	89	6,644	6,840
14	0	36	45	25	16	486	82	17	0	106	568	6,216	6,890
15	0	36	45	28	17	927	89	18	0	109	1,016	5,375	6,500
16	0	36	192	46	18	909	160	19	0	274	1,069	5,007	6,350
17	0	189	405	42	19	1,034	160	20	0	636	1,194	4,070	5,900
18	0	118	303	25	20	979	160	21	0	446	1,139	3,575	5,160
19	0	40	179	25	21	677	106	22	0	244	783	3,433	4,460
20	0	36	114	45	22	0	124	23	0	195	124	3,331	3,650
21	0	53	107	70	23	126	124	24	0	230	250	3,270	3,750
22	0	82	125	53	24	1,053	106	25	0	260	1,159	2,931	4,350
23	0	73	200	43	25	615	89	26	0	316	704	2,930	3,950
24	0	36	200	60	26	546	106	27	0	296	652	3,712	4,660
25	0	36	200	53	27	344	113	28	0	289	457	5,394	6,140
26	0	36	200	25	28	246	124	29	0	261	370	5,659	6,290
27	0	87	263	25	29	0	230	30	0	375	230	5,155	5,760
28	0	155	405	40	30	0	53	31	0	600	53	4,197	4,850
Total	0	1,686	3,731	1,012	Total	16,447	5,457	Total	0	6,429	21,904	183,547	211,880

Col. 2 - 24 hours beginning 1200 of date shown.
Col. 3 - 24 hours ending 2400 one day later.
Col. 4 - 24 hours beginning 1500 one day later.
Col. 5 - 24 hours beginning 0800 of date shown.
Col. 6 - 24 hours beginning 1600 of date shown.

Col. 7 = Col. 2 + Col. 3 + Col. 4 in response to direction (Col. 1).
Col. 8 = Col. 2 + Col. 3 + Col. 4 - Col. 7.
Col. 9 = Col. 5 + Col. 6.
Col. 10 = Col. 11 - Col. 7 - Col. 8 - Col. 9.
Col. 11 = 24 hours of calendar day shown.

Table 9. Controlled releases from reservoirs in the upper Delaware River Basin and segregation of flow of Delaware River at Montague, New Jersey—Continued.
(River Master daily operation record)

[Mean discharge in cubic feet per second for 24 hours; Col., Column; Cumul., Cumulative]

Controlled Releases from New York City Reservoirs					Controlled Releases from Power Reservoirs			Segregation of Flow, Delaware River at Montague, New Jersey							
Directed		Pepacton	Cannonsville	Neversink		Lake Wallenpaupack	Rio Reservoir		Controlled Releases			Computed uncontrolled	Total	Excess Release Credits	
Date 2004	Amount				Date 2004			Date 2004	New York City Reservoirs		Power-plants			Daily	Cumul.
									Directed	Other					
Date 2004	Col. 1	Col. 2	Col. 3	Col. 4	2004	Col. 5	Col. 6	2004	Col. 7	Col. 8	Col. 9	Col. 10	Col. 11	Col. 12	Col. 13
May 29	0	135	364	53	May 31	36	124	June 1	0	552	160	4,058	4,770		
30	0	96	303	46	June 1	337	124	2	0	445	461	4,574	5,480		
31	0	76	271	25	2	252	131	3	0	372	383	4,875	5,630		
June 1	0	142	277	25	3	321	142	4	0	444	463	4,623	5,530		
2	0	150	288	36	4	273	124	5	0	474	397	3,919	4,790		
3	0	118	303	45	5	0	124	6	0	466	124	3,640	4,230		
4	0	43	282	70	6	25	319	7	0	395	344	3,681	4,420		
5	0	37	260	70	7	331	220	8	0	367	551	3,322	4,240		
6	0	36	231	73	8	604	199	9	0	340	803	2,827	3,970		
7	0	36	308	90	9	619	131	10	0	434	750	2,716	3,900		
8	0	68	430	34	10	335	106	11	0	532	441	2,367	3,340		
9	0	53	309	90	11	375	152	12	0	452	527	2,121	3,100		
10	0	36	308	90	12	0	0	13	0	434	0	1,906	2,340		
11	0	37	274	90	13	29	0	14	0	401	29	1,710	2,140		
12	0	71	195	93	14	367	152	15	0	359	519	1,442	2,320		
13	0	93	155	108	15	285	0	16	0	356	285	1,549	2,190	0	0
14	114	108	155	108	16	302	0	17	114	257	302	1,597	2,270	114	114
15	171	108	176	108	17	381	0	18	171	221	381	2,077	2,850	171	285
16	204	108	217	71	18	315	0	19	204	192	315	2,189	2,900	204	489
17	617	108	486	29	19	0	0	20	623	0	0	1,707	2,330	580	1,069
18	0	108	218	57	20	34	0	21	0	383	34	1,383	1,800	50	1,119
19	0	119	215	42	21	279	0	22	0	376	279	1,305	1,960	70	1,189
20	75	130	187	62	22	256	0	23	75	304	256	1,235	1,870	70	1,259
21	144	138	189	76	23	315	0	24	144	259	315	1,132	1,850	70	1,329
22	305	139	200	82	24	323	0	25	305	116	323	1,076	1,820	70	1,399
23	264	139	227	88	25	275	0	26	264	190	275	1,031	1,760	10	1,409
24	376	139	190	88	26	0	71	27	376	41	71	1,262	1,750	0	1,409
25	600	139	399	79	27	0	0	28	600	17	0	1,333	1,950	183	1,592
26	325	121	187	88	28	177	0	29	325	71	177	1,207	1,780	30	1,622
27	380	139	187	88	29	229	0	30	380	34	229	1,057	1,700	-50	1,572
Total	3,575	2,970	7,791	2,104		7,075	2,119		3,581	9,284	9,194	68,921	90,980		

Col. 2 - 24 hours beginning 1200 of date shown.
Col. 3 - 24 hours ending 2400 one day later.
Col. 4 - 24 hours beginning 1500 one day later.
Col. 5 - 24 hours beginning 0800 of date shown.
Col. 6 - 24 hours beginning 1600 of date shown.

Col. 7 = Col. 2 + Col. 3 + Col. 4 in response to direction (Col. 1).
Col. 8 = Col. 2 + Col. 3 + Col. 4 - Col. 7.
Col. 9 = Col. 5 + Col. 6.
Col. 10 = Col. 11 - Col. 7 - Col. 8 - Col. 9.
Col. 11 = 24 hours of calendar day shown.

Col. 12 = Col. 11 - Col. 8 - 1,750 ft³/s computed arithmetically, but not greater than Col. 7; except that part of Col. 8 contributing to the excess-release increment of Col. 11.

Col. 13 = Season limit of cumulative credit beginning June 15, 2004 = 13,556 (ft³/s)·d. A total of 7,856 (ft³/s)·d is available for release.

Table 9. Controlled releases from reservoirs in the upper Delaware River Basin and segregation of flow of Delaware River at Montague, New Jersey—Continued. (River Master daily operation record)

[Mean discharge in cubic feet per second for 24 hours; Col., Column; Cumul., Cumulative]

Controlled Releases from New York City Reservoirs

Date 2004	Directed Amount Col. 1	Pepacton Col. 2	Cannonsville Col. 3	Neversink Col. 4
June 28	743	139	512	88
29	583	139	357	90
30	629	166	371	104
July 1	1,002	186	712	104
2	1,030	186	739	104
3	1,107	186	818	104
4	903	186	614	104
5	920	186	645	88
6	718	170	449	99
7	544	179	316	99
8	1,074	181	783	110
9	1,009	181	699	110
10	743	181	452	110
11	665	181	376	110
12	399	181	309	110
13	370	181	309	93
14	358	166	309	93
15	0	162	308	93
16	0	162	309	93
17	0	162	309	93
18	0	162	312	93
19	0	128	399	93
20	0	124	630	93
21	0	136	580	93
22	0	145	399	82
23	0	147	316	53
24	0	164	316	53
25	0	170	316	50
26	0	167	186	25
27	0	36	63	25
28	0	36	62	25
Total	12,797	4,876	13,275	2,684

Controlled Releases from Power Reservoirs

Date 2004	Lake Wallenpaupack Col. 5	Rio Reservoir Col. 6
June 30	231	0
July 1	184	0
2	147	0
3	0	0
4	0	0
5	1	0
6	337	43
7	457	0
8	280	0
9	378	71
10	0	0
11	6	0
12	250	0
13	373	0
14	349	0
15	290	0
16	521	0
17	0	0
18	4	0
19	286	0
20	264	0
21	279	0
22	355	0
23	299	0
24	348	71
25	398	89
26	498	57
27	1,113	0
28	703	184
29	807	330
30	742	113
Total	9,900	958

Segregation of Flow, Delaware River at Montague, New Jersey

Date 2004	Controlled Releases — New York City Reservoirs Directed Col. 7	Controlled Releases — New York City Reservoirs Other Col. 8	Controlled Releases — Power-plants Col. 9	Computed uncontrolled Col. 10	Total Col. 11	Excess Release Credits Daily Col. 12	Excess Release Credits Cumul. Col. 13
July 1	739	0	231	870	1,840	90	1,662
2	586	0	184	940	1,710	-40	1,622
3	641	0	147	802	1,590	-160	1,462
4	1,002	0	0	698	1,700	-50	1,412
5	1,029	0	0	711	1,740	-10	1,402
6	1,108	0	1	681	1,790	40	1,442
7	904	0	380	866	2,150	400	1,842
8	919	0	457	954	2,330	580	2,422
9	718	0	280	1,222	2,220	470	2,892
10	544	50	449	1,037	2,080	330	3,222
11	1,074	0	0	796	1,870	120	3,342
12	990	0	6	744	1,740	-10	3,332
13	743	0	250	1,017	2,010	260	3,592
14	667	0	373	1,130	2,170	420	4,012
15	399	201	349	1,461	2,410	399	4,411
16	370	213	290	2,577	3,450	370	4,781
17	358	210	521	2,271	3,360	358	5,139
18	0	563	0	1,987	2,550	0	5,139
19	0	564	4	2,122	2,690	0	5,139
20	0	564	286	2,750	3,600	0	5,139
21	0	567	264	2,279	3,110	0	5,139
22	0	620	279	1,871	2,770	0	5,139
23	0	847	355	1,488	2,690	0	5,139
24	0	809	299	3,532	4,640	0	5,139
25	0	626	419	3,505	4,550	0	5,139
26	0	516	487	2,387	3,390	0	5,139
27	0	533	555	1,922	3,010	0	5,139
28	0	536	1,113	9,151	10,800	0	5,139
29	0	378	887	10,635	11,900	0	5,139
30	0	124	1,137	8,659	9,920	0	5,139
31	0	123	855	5,452	6,430	0	5,139
Total	12,791	8,044	10,858	76,517	108,210		

Col. 2 - 24 hours beginning 1200 of date shown.
Col. 3 - 24 hours ending 2400 one day later.
Col. 4 - 24 hours beginning 1500 one day later.
Col. 5 - 24 hours beginning 0800 of date shown.
Col. 6 - 24 hours beginning 1600 of date shown.

Col. 7 = Col. 2 + Col. 3 + Col. 4 in response to direction (Col. 1).
Col. 8 = Col. 2 + Col. 3 + Col. 4 - Col. 7.
Col. 9 = Col. 5 + Col. 6.
Col. 10 = Col. 11 - Col. 7 - Col. 8 - Col. 9.
Col. 11 = 24 hours of calendar day shown.

Col. 12 = Col. 11 - Col. 8 - 1,750 ft³/s computed arithmetically, but not greater than Col. 7; except that part of Col. 8 contributing to the excess-release increment of Col. 11.

Col. 13 = Season limit of cumulative credit beginning June 15, 2004 = 13,556 (ft³/s)·d. A total of 7,856 (ft³/s)·d is available for release.

Table 9. Controlled releases from reservoirs in the upper Delaware River Basin and segregation of flow of Delaware River at Montague, New Jersey—Continued.
(River Master daily operation record)

[Mean discharge in cubic feet per second for 24 hours; Col., Column; Cumul., Cumulative]

Controlled Releases from New York City Reservoirs					Controlled Releases from Power Reservoirs			Segregation of Flow, Delaware River at Montague, New Jersey							
Directed		Pepacton	Cannonsville	Neversink		Lake Wallenpaupack	Rio Reservoir		Controlled Releases			Computed uncontrolled	Total	Excess Release Credits	
Date 2004	Amount				Date 2004			Date 2004	New York City Reservoirs Directed	Other	Power-plants			Daily	Cumul.
	Col. 1	Col. 2	Col. 3	Col. 4		Col. 5	Col. 6		Col. 7	Col. 8	Col. 9	Col. 10	Col. 11	Col. 12	Col. 13
July 29	0	36	62	25	July 31	501	0	Aug. 1	0	123	501	4,446	5,070	0	5,139
30	0	36	62	25	Aug. 1	419	195	2	0	123	614	4,773	5,510	0	5,139
31	0	36	62	25	2	578	319	3	0	123	897	3,970	4,990	0	5,139
Aug. 1	0	36	102	46	3	580	284	4	0	184	864	3,132	4,180	0	5,139
2	0	36	159	125	4	439	35	5	0	320	474	2,886	3,680	0	5,139
3	0	36	220	105	5	310	0	6	0	361	310	3,229	3,900	0	5,139
4	0	36	210	46	6	398	167	7	0	292	565	2,653	3,510	0	5,139
5	0	36	125	28	7	0	0	8	0	189	0	2,211	2,400	0	5,139
6	0	36	102	39	8	1	0	9	0	177	1	1,922	2,100	0	5,139
7	0	36	113	54	9	400	0	10	0	203	400	1,747	2,350	0	5,139
8	0	53	124	76	10	451	0	11	0	253	451	1,716	2,420	0	5,139
9	0	87	124	84	11	535	35	12	0	295	570	1,895	2,760	0	5,139
10	70	107	130	63	12	870	562	13	70	230	1,432	30,568	32,300	70	5,209
11	0	107	138	36	13	1,459	1,465	14	0	281	2,924	25,695	28,900	0	5,209
12	0	99	88	25	14	1,618	1,273	15	0	212	2,891	13,197	16,300	0	5,209
13	0	36	60	25	15	1,618	691	16	0	121	2,309	11,270	13,700	0	5,209
14	0	36	59	25	16	1,515	266	17	0	120	1,781	13,299	15,200	0	5,209
15	0	36	59	54	17	1,392	532	18	0	149	1,924	10,927	13,000	0	5,209
16	0	580	60	212	18	1,574	426	19	0	852	2,000	7,648	10,500	0	5,209
17	0	96	101	215	19	1,553	337	20	0	412	1,890	6,868	9,170	0	5,209
18	0	657	153	184	20	867	0	21	0	994	867	6,869	8,730	0	5,209
19	0	739	312	46	21	499	528	22	0	1,097	1,027	8,276	10,400	0	5,209
20	0	732	577	119	22	440	791	23	0	1,428	1,231	6,091	8,750	0	5,209
21	0	467	756	50	23	449	323	24	0	1,273	772	4,715	6,760	0	5,209
22	0	470	849	25	24	550	89	25	0	1,344	639	3,767	5,750	0	5,209
23	0	347	893	28	25	534	106	26	0	1,268	640	3,452	5,360	0	5,209
24	0	531	954	39	26	393	124	27	0	1,524	517	2,849	4,890	0	5,209
25	0	650	777	50	27	606	142	28	0	1,477	748	2,365	4,590	0	5,209
26	0	656	681	65	28	476	35	29	0	1,402	511	2,157	4,070	0	5,209
27	0	439	622	70	29	513	18	30	0	1,131	531	2,878	4,540	0	5,209
28	0	459	608	70	30	656	294	31	0	1,137	950	6,033	8,120	0	5,209
Total	70	7,744	9,342	2,079		22,194	9,037		70	19,095	31,231	203,504	253,900	70	

Col. 2 - 24 hours beginning 1200 of date shown.
Col. 3 - 24 hours ending 2400 one day later.
Col. 4 - 24 hours beginning 1500 one day later.
Col. 5 - 24 hours beginning 0800 of date shown.
Col. 6 - 24 hours beginning 1600 of date shown.

Col. 7 = Col. 2 + Col. 3 + Col. 4 in response to direction (Col. 1).
Col. 8 = Col. 2 + Col. 3 + Col. 4 - Col. 7.
Col. 9 = Col. 5 + Col. 6.
Col. 10 = Col. 11 - Col. 7 - Col. 8 - Col. 9.
Col. 11 = 24 hours of calendar day shown.

Col. 12 = Col. 11 - Col. 8 - 1,750 ft³/s computed arithmetically, but not greater than Col. 7; except that part of Col. 8 contributing to the excess-release increment of Col. 11.

Col. 13 = Season limit of cumulative credit beginning June 15, 2004 = 13,556 (ft³/s)·d. A total of 7,856 (ft³/s)·d is available for release.

Table 9. Controlled releases from reservoirs in the upper Delaware River Basin and segregation of flow of Delaware River at Montague, New Jersey—Continued.
(River Master daily operation record)

[Mean discharge in cubic feet per second for 24 hours; Col., Column; Cumul., Cumulative; e, estimated]

Controlled Releases from New York City Reservoirs					Controlled Releases from Power Reservoirs			Segregation of Flow, Delaware River at Montague, New Jersey							
Directed		Pepacton	Cannonsville	Neversink		Lake Wallenpaupack	Rio Reservoir		Controlled Releases New York City Reservoirs		Power-plants	Computed uncontrolled	Total	Excess Release Credits	
Amount					Date			Date	Directed	Other				Daily	Cumul.
Date 2004	Col. 1	Col. 2	Col. 3	Col. 4	2004	Col. 5	Col. 6	2004	Col. 7	Col. 8	Col. 9	Col. 10	Col. 11	Col. 12	Col. 13
Aug. 29	0	511	350	70	Aug. 31	584	1,220	Sept. 1	0	931	1,804	6,155	8,890	0	5,209
30	0	511	251	62	Sept. 1	568	833	2	0	824	1,401	4,475	6,700	0	5,209
31	0	504	401	25	2	602	550	3	0	930	1,152	3,198	5,280	0	5,209
Sept. 1	0	364	444	25	3	616	270	4	0	833	886	2,651	4,370	0	5,209
2	0	261	429	34	4	377	0	5	0	724	377	2,309	3,410	0	5,209
3	0	125	367	25	5	280	0	6	0	517	280	2,143	2,940	0	5,209
4	0	155	323	25	6	299	71	7	0	503	370	1,967	2,840	0	5,209
5	0	155	300	25	7	489	184	8	0	480	673	2,077	3,230	0	5,209
6	0	155	235	25	8	703	316	9	0	415	1,019	5,806	7,240	0	5,209
7	0	170	217	25	9	898	770	10	0	412	1,668	12,120	14,200	0	5,209
8	0	162	537	25	10	1,049	748	11	0	724	1,797	9,279	11,800	0	5,209
9	0	36	1,236	25	11	852	280	12	0	1,297	1,132	6,411	8,840	0	5,209
10	0	37	1,250	25	12	983	117	13	0	1,312	1,100	4,698	7,110	0	5,209
11	0	57	896	25	13	880	461	14	0	978	1,341	3,791	6,110	0	5,209
12	0	90	709	25	14	856	443	15	0	824	1,299	3,357	5,480	0	5,209
13	0	118	586	25	15	937	195	16	0	729	1,132	3,029	4,890	0	5,209
14	0	131	487	32	16	991	443	17	0	650	1,434	2,776	4,860	0	5,209
15	0	135	441	25	17	1,008	706	18	0	601	1,714	79,885	82,200	0	5,209
16	0	139	402	25	18	992	2,489	19	0	566	3,481	111,953	116,000	0	5,209
17	0	107	178	25	19	1,603	7,996	20	0	310	9,599	39,291	49,200	0	5,209
18	0	36	57	25	20	1,547	4,504	21	0	118	6,051	24,831	31,000	0	5,209
19	0	36	54	25	21	1,560	2,812	22	0	115	4,372	17,613	22,100	0	5,209
20	0	36	45	25	22	1,566	1,582	23	0	106	3,148	13,546	16,800	0	5,209
21	0	36	46	25	23	1,563	801	24	0	107	2,364	11,529	14,000	0	5,209
22	0	36	266	25	24	1,557	447	25	0	327	2,004	10,069	12,400	0	5,209
23	0	565	1,538	25	25	647	0	26	0	2,128	647	5,925	e8,700	0	5,209
24	0	741	1,539	25	26	858	106	27	0	2,305	964	4,531	e7,800	0	5,209
25	0	741	1,538	25	27	827	539	28	0	2,304	1,366	4,930	e8,600	0	5,209
26	0	736	1,129	25	28	871	1,152	29	0	1,890	2,023	16,187	20,100	0	5,209
27	0	599	815	25	29	799	1,340	30	0	1,439	2,139	14,922	18,500	0	5,209
Total	0	7,485	17,066	848		27,362	31,375		0	25,399	58,737	431,454	515,590	0	

Col. 2 - 24 hours beginning 1200 of date shown.
Col. 3 - 24 hours ending 2400 one day later.
Col. 4 - 24 hours beginning 1500 one day later.
Col. 5 - 24 hours beginning 0800 of date shown.
Col. 6 - 24 hours beginning 1600 of date shown.

Col. 7 = Col. 2 + Col. 3 + Col. 4 in response to direction (Col. 1).
Col. 8 = Col. 2 + Col. 3 + Col. 4 - Col. 7.
Col. 9 = Col. 5 + Col. 6.
Col. 10 = Col. 11 - Col. 7 - Col. 8 - Col. 9.
Col. 11 = 24 hours of calendar day shown.

Col. 12 = Col. 11 - Col. 8 - 1,750 ft³/s computed arithmetically, but not greater than Col. 7; except that part of Col. 8 contributing to the excess-release increment of Col. 11.

Col. 13 = Season limit of cumulative credit beginning June 15, 2004 = 13,556 (ft³/s)·d. A total of 7,856 (ft³/s)·d is available for release.

Table 9. Controlled releases from reservoirs in the upper Delaware River Basin and segregation of flow of Delaware River at Montague, New Jersey—Continued.

(River Master daily operation record)

[Mean discharge in cubic feet per second for 24 hours; Col., Column; Cumul., Cumulative]

Controlled Releases from New York City Reservoirs					Controlled Releases from Power Reservoirs			Segregation of Flow, Delaware River at Montague, New Jersey							
Directed		Pepacton	Cannonsville	Neversink	Date	Lake Wallenpaupack	Rio Reservoir	Date	Controlled Releases			Computed uncontrolled	Total	Excess Release Credits	
Date 2004	Amount				2004			2004	New York City Reservoirs		Power-plants			Daily	Cumul.
									Directed	Other					
	Col. 1	Col. 2	Col. 3	Col. 4		Col. 5	Col. 6		Col. 7	Col. 8	Col. 9	Col. 10	Col. 11	Col. 12	Col. 13
Sept. 28	0	640	1,521	25	Sept. 30	903	773	Oct. 1	0	2,186	1,676	11,838	15,700	0	5,209
29	0	640	2,062	25	Oct. 1	886	1,337	2	0	2,727	2,223	7,850	12,800	0	5,209
30	0	340	1,637	25	2	906	779	3	0	2,002	1,685	7,813	11,500	0	5,209
Oct. 1	0	667	1,417	25	3	878	592	4	0	2,109	1,470	6,621	10,200	0	5,209
2	0	673	1,341	25	4	819	358	5	0	2,039	1,177	5,684	8,900	0	5,209
3	0	673	1,235	25	5	821	390	6	0	1,933	1,211	4,726	7,870	0	5,209
4	0	673	1,036	25	6	827	191	7	0	1,734	1,018	4,208	6,960	0	5,209
5	0	639	900	25	7	827	578	8	0	1,564	1,405	3,801	6,770	0	5,209
6	0	671	767	25	8	906	454	9	0	1,463	1,360	3,097	5,920	0	5,209
7	0	653	370	25	9	904	702	10	0	1,048	1,606	2,496	5,150	0	5,209
8	0	108	42	25	10	906	496	11	0	175	1,402	2,993	4,570	0	5,209
9	0	107	73	37	11	829	252	12	0	217	1,081	3,012	4,310	0	5,209
10	0	162	82	37	12	896	188	13	0	281	1,084	2,745	4,110	0	5,209
11	0	162	57	32	13	891	99	14	0	251	990	2,659	3,900	0	5,209
12	0	169	45	42	14	900	0	15	0	256	900	2,634	3,790	0	5,209
13	0	187	45	56	15	829	18	16	0	288	847	3,175	4,310	0	5,209
14	0	186	45	39	16	832	383	17	0	270	1,215	4,305	5,790	0	5,209
15	0	186	45	25	17	734	103	18	0	256	837	3,607	4,700	0	5,209
16	0	186	45	25	18	498	103	19	0	256	601	4,143	5,000	0	5,209
17	0	186	45	25	19	499	71	20	0	256	570	10,174	11,000	0	5,209
18	0	181	45	25	20	492	181	21	0	251	673	7,666	8,590	0	5,209
19	0	104	45	25	21	468	170	22	0	174	638	6,158	6,970	0	5,209
20	0	82	45	25	22	625	287	23	0	152	912	5,456	6,520	0	5,209
21	0	77	45	25	23	644	206	24	0	147	850	4,853	5,850	0	5,209
22	0	62	45	25	24	858	57	25	0	132	915	4,623	5,670	0	5,209
23	0	63	45	25	25	965	0	26	0	133	965	4,342	5,440	0	5,209
24	0	77	45	25	26	1,048	0	27	0	147	1,048	3,975	5,170	0	5,209
25	0	77	45	25	27	467	113	28	0	147	580	3,793	4,520	0	5,209
26	0	93	45	25	28	502	64	29	0	163	566	3,691	4,420	0	5,209
27	0	93	45	25	29	417	138	30	0	163	555	3,412	4,130	0	5,209
28	0	107	45	25	30	0	0	31	0	177	0	3,683	3,860	0	5,209
Total	0	8,924	13,305	868		22,977	9,083		0	23,097	32,060	149,233	204,390		

Col. 2 - 24 hours beginning 1200 of date shown.
Col. 3 - 24 hours ending 2400 one day later.
Col. 4 - 24 hours beginning 1500 one day later.
Col. 5 - 24 hours beginning 0800 of date shown.
Col. 6 - 24 hours beginning 1600 of date shown.

Col. 7 = Col. 2 + Col. 3 + Col. 4 in response to direction (Col. 1).
Col. 8 = Col. 2 + Col. 3 + Col. 4 - Col. 7.
Col. 9 = Col. 5 + Col. 6.
Col. 10 = Col. 11 - Col. 7 - Col. 8 - Col. 9.
Col. 11 = 24 hours of calendar day shown.

Col. 12 = Col. 11 - Col. 8 - 1,750 ft³/s computed arithmetically, but not greater than Col. 7; except that part of Col. 8 contributing to the excess-release increment of Col. 11.

Col. 13 = Season limit of cumulative credit beginning June 15, 2004, of 13,556 (ft³/s)·d. A total of 7,856 (ft³/s)·d is available for release.

40

Table 9. Controlled releases from reservoirs in the upper Delaware River Basin and segregation of flow of Delaware River at Montague, New Jersey—Continued. (River Master daily operation record)

[Mean discharge in cubic feet per second for 24 hours; Col., Column; Cumul., Cumulative]

Controlled Releases from New York City Reservoirs					Controlled Releases from Power Reservoirs			Segregation of Flow, Delaware River at Montague, New Jersey							
Directed		Pepacton	Cannonsville	Neversink		Lake Wallenpaupack	Rio Reservoir		Controlled Releases			Computed uncontrolled	Total	Excess Release Credits	
Date	Amount				Date			Date	New York City Reservoirs		Power-plants			Daily	Cumul.
2004	Col. 1	Col. 2	Col. 3	Col. 4	2004	Col. 5	Col. 6	2004	Directed Col. 7	Other Col. 8	Col. 9	Col. 10	Col. 11	Col. 12	Col. 13
Oct. 29	0	108	46	25	Oct. 31	0	138	Nov. 1	0	179	138	3,383	3,700	0	5,209
30	0	108	45	28	Nov. 1	350	71	2	0	181	421	3,118	3,720	0	5,209
31	0	118	265	32	2	308	67	3	0	415	375	3,060	3,850	0	5,209
Nov. 1	0	118	487	32	3	219	67	4	0	637	286	2,767	3,690	0	5,209
2	0	124	430	32	4	325	199	5	0	586	524	3,460	4,570	0	5,209
3	0	124	261	31	5	305	177	6	0	416	482	3,762	4,660	0	5,209
4	0	122	65	25	6	0	0	7	0	212	0	3,538	3,750	0	5,209
5	0	42	70	25	7	0	135	8	0	137	135	3,138	3,410	0	5,209
6	0	43	70	25	8	295	337	9	0	138	632	2,890	3,660	0	5,209
7	0	102	226	25	9	347	0	10	0	353	347	2,690	3,390	0	5,209
8	0	128	175	25	10	262	0	11	0	328	262	2,510	3,100	0	5,209
9	0	128	116	25	11	294	0	12	0	269	294	2,597	3,160	0	5,209
10	0	128	60	28	12	506	0	13	0	216	506	2,578	3,300	0	5,209
11	0	128	79	37	13	0	0	14	0	244	0	2,676	2,920	0	5,209
12	0	125	68	25	14	0	0	15	0	218	0	2,572	2,790	0	5,209
13	0	94	54	25	15	245	0	16	0	173	245	2,582	3,000	0	5,209
14	0	124	56	39	16	568	89	17	0	219	657	2,434	3,310	0	5,209
15	0	139	46	42	17	312	113	18	0	227	425	2,518	3,170	0	5,209
16	0	138	45	56	18	583	71	19	0	239	654	2,337	3,230	0	5,209
17	0	136	45	70	19	281	85	20	0	251	366	2,403	3,020	0	5,209
18	0	138	45	68	20	0	85	21	0	251	85	2,464	2,800	0	5,209
19	0	139	45	68	21	0	156	22	0	252	156	2,512	2,920	0	5,209
20	0	139	45	68	22	385	301	23	0	252	686	2,462	3,400	0	5,209
21	0	139	45	70	23	261	294	24	0	254	555	2,471	3,280	0	5,209
22	0	139	45	70	24	295	298	25	0	254	593	3,023	3,870	0	5,209
23	0	139	45	59	25	0	301	26	0	243	301	5,596	6,140	0	5,209
24	0	136	45	50	26	0	301	27	0	231	301	5,718	6,250	0	5,209
25	0	105	45	42	27	0	301	28	0	192	301	10,407	10,900	0	5,209
26	0	85	46	36	28	7	298	29	0	167	305	32,728	33,200	0	5,209
27	0	54	46	25	29	1,070	418	30	0	125	1,488	19,687	21,300	0	5,209
Total	0	3,490	3,161	1,208		7,218	4,302		0	7,859	11,520	144,081	163,460		

Col. 2 - 24 hours beginning 1200 of date shown.
Col. 3 - 24 hours ending 2400 one day later.
Col. 4 - 24 hours beginning 1500 one day later.
Col. 5 - 24 hours beginning 0800 of date shown.
Col. 6 - 24 hours beginning 1600 of date shown.

Col. 7 = Col. 2 + Col. 3 + Col. 4 in response to direction (Col. 1).
Col. 8 = Col. 2 + Col. 3 + Col. 4 - Col. 7.
Col. 9 = Col. 5 + Col. 6.
Col. 10 = Col. 11 - Col. 7 - Col. 8 - Col. 9.
Col. 11 = 24 hours of calendar day shown.

Col. 12 = Col. 11 - Col. 8 - 1,750 ft³/s computed arithmetically, but not greater than Col. 7; except that part of Col. 8 contributing to the excess-release increment of Col. 11.

Col. 13 = Season limit of cumulative credit beginning June 15, 2004 = 13,556 (ft³/s)·d. A total of 7,856 (ft³/s)·d is available for release.

Table 10. Diversions to New York City water-supply system. (River Master daily operation record)

[Million gallons per day for 24-hour period beginning 0800 local time]

Date 2003	East Delaware Tunnel	West Delaware Tunnel	Neversink Tunnel	Average June 1, 2003, to date	Date 2004	East Delaware Tunnel	West Delaware Tunnel	Neversink Tunnel	Average June 1, 2003, to date
Dec. 1	388	0	10	511	Jan. 1	289	0	0	476
2	446	0	0	511	2	459	0	0	476
3	441	0	0	510	3	495	0	0	476
4	448	0	0	510	4	500	0	0	476
5	501	0	0	510	5	500	0	0	476
6	496	0	0	510	6	495	0	0	477
7	501	0	0	510	7	500	0	0	477
8	502	0	0	510	8	500	0	0	477
9	502	0	0	510	9	500	0	0	477
10	502	0	0	510	10	499	0	0	477
11	497	0	0	509	11	499	0	0	477
12	497	0	0	509	12	499	0	0	477
13	502	0	0	509	13	499	0	0	477
14	501	0	0	509	14	499	0	0	477
15	496	0	0	509	15	499	271	0	479
16	290	0	0	508	16	499	295	0	480
17	0	0	0	506	17	493	294	0	481
18	0	0	0	503	18	438	282	0	482
19	0	0	0	501	19	492	292	0	484
20	0	0	0	498	20	498	295	0	485
21	0	0	0	496	21	393	241	0	486
22	0	0	0	493	22	497	296	0	487
23	0	0	0	491	23	468	212	0	488
24	0	0	0	489	24	496	296	0	489
25	0	0	0	486	25	496	296	0	490
26	0	0	0	484	26	496	296	0	492
27	0	0	0	482	27	495	296	0	493
28	0	0	0	479	28	495	296	0	494
29	0	0	286	478	29	495	296	0	495
30	0	0	384	478	30	491	293	0	496
31	3	0	305	477	31	496	296	0	498
Total	7,513	0	985			14,970	4,843	0	

Table 10. Diversions to New York City water-supply system—Continued. (River Master daily operation record)

[Million gallons per day for 24-hour period beginning 0800 local time]

Date 2004	East Delaware Tunnel	West Delaware Tunnel	Neversink Tunnel	Average June 1, 2003, to date	Date 2004	East Delaware Tunnel	West Delaware Tunnel	Neversink Tunnel	Average June 1, 2003, to date
Feb. 1	496	296	0	499	Mar. 1	491	195	0	525
2	496	296	0	500	2	491	195	0	526
3	496	296	0	501	3	491	195	0	526
4	496	296	0	502	4	465	196	361	528
5	495	296	0	504	5	225	31	458	529
6	495	210	0	504	6	34	26	459	529
7	495	195	0	505	7	35	25	459	529
8	495	195	0	506	8	0	26	459	528
9	495	196	0	507	9	0	0	459	528
10	495	195	0	507	10	0	0	460	528
11	495	195	0	508	11	0	0	462	528
12	494	196	0	509	12	0	0	463	528
13	494	295	0	510	13	0	0	463	527
14	494	295	0	511	14	0	0	462	527
15	494	295	0	512	15	0	0	462	527
16	494	295	0	513	16	160	0	172	526
17	494	295	0	514	17	292	0	145	526
18	493	295	0	515	18	296	0	148	526
19	493	295	0	516	19	304	0	144	525
20	493	295	0	517	20	298	0	146	525
21	493	294	0	518	21	279	0	145	525
22	493	294	0	519	22	300	0	144	524
23	493	294	0	520	23	303	0	177	524
24	493	294	0	521	24	287	0	145	524
25	493	294	0	522	25	436	0	145	524
26	493	195	0	523	26	441	0	147	524
27	492	195	0	523	27	440	0	144	525
28	492	195	0	524	28	440	0	144	525
29	491	195	0	525	29	449	0	146	525
					30	449	0	143	525
					31	449	0	145	525
Total	14,325	7,472	0			7,855	889	7,807	

Table 10. Diversions to New York City water-supply system—Continued.
(River Master daily operation record)

[Million gallons per day for 24-hour period beginning 0800 local time]

Date 2004	East Delaware Tunnel	West Delaware Tunnel	Neversink Tunnel	Average June 1, 2003, to date	Date 2004	East Delaware Tunnel	West Delaware Tunnel	Neversink Tunnel	Average June 1, 2003, to date
Apr. 1	320	0	106	525	May 1	447	0	193	520
2	300	0	97	525	2	448	0	195	521
3	292	0	95	524	3	449	0	192	521
4	255	0	97	524	4	449	0	190	521
5	271	0	105	523	5	450	0	195	522
6	0	0	0	522	6	450	0	14	522
7	17	0	156	520	7	450	0	143	522
8	362	0	168	520	8	450	0	142	522
9	433	0	118	521	9	451	0	144	522
10	452	0	110	521	10	451	0	142	522
11	452	0	107	521	11	450	0	141	523
12	447	0	103	521	12	450	0	143	523
13	452	0	105	521	13	446	0	144	523
14	0	0	368	521	14	450	0	158	523
15	0	0	384	520	15	451	0	145	523
16	290	0	212	520	16	451	0	145	524
17	281	0	210	520	17	487	97	106	524
18	299	0	210	520	18	498	97	98	525
19	299	0	161	520	19	498	97	97	525
20	299	0	190	520	20	496	97	93	526
21	299	0	203	520	21	499	147	53	526
22	296	0	246	520	22	499	146	59	526
23	449	0	99	520	23	499	146	52	527
24	451	0	189	520	24	458	198	16	527
25	453	0	14	520	25	450	286	87	528
26	454	0	104	520	26	445	292	52	529
27	260	0	353	520	27	449	39	240	529
28	0	0	385	520	28	449	0	382	530
29	0	0	381	520	29	448	0	239	531
30	448	0	203	520	30	444	0	232	531
					31	449	97	189	532
Total	8,631	0	5,279			14,261	1,739	4,421	

Table 10. Diversions to New York City water-supply system—Continued. (River Master daily operation record)

[Million gallons per day for 24-hour period beginning 0800 local time]

Date 2004	East Delaware Tunnel	West Delaware Tunnel	Neversink Tunnel	Average June 1, 2004, to date	Date 2004	East Delaware Tunnel	West Delaware Tunnel	Neversink Tunnel	Average June 1, 2004, to date
June 1	448	98	168	714	July 1	454	296	110	750
2	448	97	143	701	2	454	296	97	753
3	448	14	276	713	3	454	296	96	755
4	443	0	160	686	4	449	296	96	758
5	448	0	194	677	5	452	296	95	760
6	448	0	189	670	6	452	220	106	761
7	448	271	103	692	7	300	197	106	757
8	447	296	96	710	8	297	195	106	752
9	447	287	52	719	9	300	197	105	749
10	340	283	50	714	10	300	197	106	745
11	342	296	0	707	11	300	196	106	741
12	342	296	0	702	12	302	196	97	738
13	343	296	0	697	13	303	196	99	735
14	347	296	0	693	14	303	196	98	732
15	354	296	143	700	15	301	194	147	730
16	356	296	149	706	16	303	196	159	728
17	354	296	115	709	17	299	194	146	726
18	348	293	83	710	18	303	196	146	724
19	348	293	94	711	19	303	196	143	723
20	351	295	93	713	20	300	235	188	723
21	351	295	0	710	21	302	263	194	723
22	352	295	146	713	22	305	243	193	724
23	352	295	121	716	23	64	63	68	714
24	436	295	96	720	24	0	0	0	701
25	452	296	96	725	25	0	0	0	688
26	452	296	109	730	26	0	0	0	676
27	453	296	107	735	27	0	0	129	666
28	448	293	95	739	28	0	0	355	661
29	453	296	106	743	29	0	0	354	655
30	449	293	96	746	30	0	0	386	651
					31	0	0	385	647
Total	12,048	7,249	3,080			7,600	5,050	4,416	

Table 10. Diversions to New York City water-supply system—Continued.
(River Master daily operation record)

[Million gallons per day for 24-hour period beginning 0800 local time]

Date 2004	East Delaware Tunnel	West Delaware Tunnel	Neversink Tunnel	Average June 1, 2004, to date	East Delaware Tunnel	West Delaware Tunnel	Neversink Tunnel	Average June 1, 2004, to date	Date 2004
Aug. 1	0	0	385	642	243	0	291	564	Sept. 1
2	0	0	386	638	128	0	291	562	2
3	88	0	286	634	144	0	292	561	3
4	86	0	271	630	120	0	292	560	4
5	246	98	219	629	127	0	292	558	5
6	295	98	211	629	128	0	290	557	6
7	32	244	308	628	135	0	291	555	7
8	0	299	292	627	0	0	143	551	8
9	117	299	293	629	0	0	151	547	9
10	449	299	293	634	0	0	143	543	10
11	304	97	29	631	0	0	309	541	11
12	177	5	35	626	0	0	306	539	12
13	0	0	0	617	0	0	307	537	13
14	0	0	0	609	134	0	306	536	14
15	0	0	0	601	244	0	177	535	15
16	224	0	0	596	239	0	190	534	16
17	305	0	0	592	347	0	141	533	17
18	310	0	0	589	0	0	0	528	18
19	302	0	0	585	0	0	0	524	19
20	136	0	301	583	0	0	0	519	20
21	126	0	291	581	0	0	278	517	21
22	125	0	290	579	0	0	289	515	22
23	134	0	310	578	383	0	363	517	23
24	132	0	306	576	348	0	384	519	24
25	132	0	298	574	0	0	384	517	25
26	133	0	306	573	0	0	385	516	26
27	1	0	263	569	212	0	385	517	27
28	0	149	147	566	27	0	142	514	28
29	0	151	210	564	0	0	311	512	29
30	215	149	96	563	0	0	384	511	30
31	295	150	243	564					
Total	4,364	2,038	6,069		2,959	0	7,517		

46

Table 10. Diversions to New York City water-supply system—Continued. (River Master daily operation record)

[Million gallons per day for 24-hour period beginning 0800 local time]

Date 2004	East Delaware Tunnel	West Delaware Tunnel	Neversink Tunnel	Average June 1, 2004, to date	Date 2004	East Delaware Tunnel	West Delaware Tunnel	Neversink Tunnel	Average June 1, 2004, to date
Oct. 1	0	0	384	510	Nov. 1	0	0	0	490
2	0	0	385	509	2	0	0	0	487
3	0	0	356	508	3	0	0	0	483
4	0	0	0	504	4	314	187	239	485
5	0	0	0	500	5	496	301	383	489
6	0	0	0	496	6	496	301	388	494
7	267	0	0	494	7	484	279	349	498
8	485	0	299	497	8	494	431	0	500
9	488	0	384	500	9	496	488	0	503
10	206	0	352	500	10	464	34	0	503
11	0	0	0	496	11	491	0	0	503
12	0	0	0	493	12	496	0	259	505
13	0	0	0	489	13	496	0	390	507
14	262	0	209	489	14	496	0	342	509
15	479	0	384	491	15	472	0	371	511
16	480	0	384	494	16	463	0	223	512
17	443	0	350	496	17	463	0	213	513
18	0	0	0	493	18	446	0	263	514
19	0	0	0	489	19	449	0	254	515
20	0	0	0	486	20	449	0	295	517
21	327	0	253	486	21	444	0	294	518
22	498	101	385	490	22	444	0	294	519
23	498	0	385	493	23	449	0	296	520
24	454	0	353	495	24	449	0	296	522
25	0	0	0	491	25	450	0	295	523
26	0	0	0	488	26	449	0	296	524
27	0	0	0	485	27	449	0	296	525
28	307	0	222	485	28	449	0	72	525
29	498	0	384	488	29	26	0	0	523
30	497	0	385	490	30	0	0	0	520
31	498	0	385	493					
Total	6,687	101	6,239			11,574	2,021	6,108	

47

Table 11. Daily mean discharge, East Branch Delaware River at Downsville, New York (station number 01417000), for report year ending November 30, 2004. (U.S. Geological Survey published record)

[All values except total are in cubic feet per second, ft³/s; total in cubic feet per second days, (ft³/s)-d; e, estimated]

DAY	DEC	JAN	FEB	MAR	APR	MAY	JUNE	JULY	AUG	SEPT	OCT	NOV
1	1,900	1,370	41	40	40	621	369	164	41	419	1,670	102
2	1,280	984	41	40	40	421	475	172	41	305	1,540	110
3	890	744	41	40	40	532	361	172	41	161	1,350	112
4	609	750	41	40	39	429	227	172	42	136	1,170	113
5	458	859	85	40	40	352	131	173	42	142	993	80
6	356	883	41	41	152	336	94	165	42	142	884	39
7	243	771	41	41	490	257	58	163	42	151	780	70
8	151	727	e40	41	577	188	51	169	46	158	357	107
9	86	769	e39	41	352	155	63	169	66	89	93	118
10	79	815	e38	41	185	95	38	170	98	40	129	119
11	593	814	e38	41	92	111	38	170	103	45	148	118
12	2,230	812	e38	40	52	102	50	170	103	67	148	119
13	1,910	812	e38	40	97	189	73	170	64	97	167	100
14	1,450	813	e38	651	321	427	91	164	41	117	171	99
15	1,210	813	e38	487	657	381	98	154	42	122	172	121
16	867	811	e38	40	699	367	98	154	1,630	131	171	127
17	1,060	748	38	40	520	346	98	154	2,810	103	171	126
18	1,590	505	38	39	454	195	98	154	2,270	12,400	172	126
19	1,650	49	38	39	434	144	102	139	1,770	10,500	129	127
20	1,610	41	38	39	408	65	114	115	1,270	4,680	83	128
21	1,300	41	38	39	350	43	121	121	1,140	2,770	71	127
22	1,130	41	38	39	281	62	125	134	1,170	1,930	61	127
23	1,040	e41	38	39	350	75	125	139	876	1,540	56	127
24	2,790	e41	39	40	298	49	125	145	793	1,200	65	127
25	6,110	e41	39	40	214	38	125	161	802	855	71	111
26	4,140	e41	39	40	484	39	116	162	710	819	80	89
27	2,860	e41	39	40	824	176	120	97	522	739	87	64
28	2,220	41	40	40	1,110	467	126	41	434	782	92	41
29	1,760	41	40	40	1,230	454	126	41	476	1,680	98	40
30	1,650	41		39	1,060	345	138	41	499	1,590	98	40
31	1,630	41		40		244		41	500		98	
Total	46,852	15,341	1,178	2,297	11,890	7,705	3,974	4,356	18,526	43,910	11,375	3,054
Mean	1,511	495	40.6	74.1	396	249	132	141	598	1,464	367	102

Year total 170,458 (ft³/s)-d

Mean 466 ft³/s

48

Table 12. Daily mean discharge, West Branch Delaware River at Stilesville, New York (station number 01425000), for report year ending November 30, 2004. (U.S. Geological Survey published record)

[All values except total are in cubic feet per second, ft³/s; total in cubic feet per second days, (ft³/s)-d; e, estimated]

DAY	DEC	JAN	FEB	MAR	APR	MAY	JUNE	JULY	AUG	SEPT	OCT	NOV
1	2,080	1,750	e94	179	1,660	1,080	972	356	72	376	1,920	815
2	1,950	1,490	e103	166	1,640	1,030	991	676	84	427	1,620	953
3	1,760	1,410	e96	128	1,560	1,330	1,030	726	154	409	1,510	771
4	1,540	1,660	e103	89	1,460	1,450	1,060	811	209	344	1,380	520
5	1,390	1,940	e96	61	1,310	1,400	962	589	215	302	1,180	278
6	1,290	2,040	90	74	1,190	1,370	886	621	136	287	1,020	240
7	1,180	1,860	125	1,900	1,090	1,300	778	436	109	238	872	207
8	1,070	1,660	123	3,150	1,020	1,190	662	308	113	223	433	298
9	984	1,480	120	3,120	936	1,080	592	793	125	573	75	216
10	912	1,190	123	2,670	848	1,030	385	688	126	1,380	144	141
11	1,290	1,020	132	2,290	790	1,100	335	438	130	1,310	259	78
12	3,010	976	137	2,000	712	1,080	275	366	138	906	284	112
13	3,190	1,000	137	1,710	777	1,090	200	303	116	693	311	182
14	2,810	936	138	1,480	1,060	982	154	307	75	565	341	222
15	2,490	801	147	1,290	1,230	903	153	306	68	471	376	268
16	2,130	548	152	1,200	1,210	887	174	305	68	428	507	291
17	1,890	383	159	1,120	1,160	951	208	304	68	399	500	314
18	2,020	317	161	1,050	1,110	918	471	305	81	4,510	477	330
19	1,960	272	164	936	1,100	697	215	304	150	9,620	596	343
20	1,750	227	170	860	1,100	485	216	390	289	6,910	771	353
21	1,530	193	191	923	1,030	419	188	605	555	4,420	834	363
22	1,370	158	221	936	956	392	188	557	753	3,530	862	369
23	1,280	131	193	885	931	396	198	385	865	2,830	882	365
24	1,860	113	148	836	932	428	227	309	941	3,280	876	364
25	4,880	86	142	872	887	415	192	309	971	2,420	852	466
26	4,970	66	147	989	985	371	392	311	768	2,020	814	804
27	4,000	56	163	1,230	1,220	581	188	222	661	1,440	776	948
28	3,150	76	164	1,690	1,240	1,250	189	90	591	1,050	727	1,560
29	2,650	100	175	1,880	1,200	1,410	480	77	575	2,160	674	3,170
30	2,180	80		1,840	1,150	1,230	351	72	345	2,500	641	3,170
31	1,960	e90		1,730		1,060		72	230		615	
Total	66,526	24,109	4,114	39,284	33,494	29,305	13,312	12,341	9,781	56,021	23,129	18,511
Mean	2,146	778	142	1,267	1,116	945	444	398	316	1,867	746	617

Year total 329,927 (ft³/s)-d

Mean 901 ft³/s

Table 13. Daily mean discharge, Neversink River at Neversink, New York (station number 01436000), for report year ending November 30, 2004.

[All values except total are in cubic feet per second, ft³/s; total in cubic feet per second days, (ft³/s)-d; e, estimated]

DAY	DEC	JAN	FEB	MAR	APR	MAY	JUNE	JULY	AUG	SEPT	OCT	NOV
1	51	43	e110	39	24	26	38	97	27	45	19	29
2	181	55	e110	72	25	27	28	104	27	26	19	36
3	283	282	e110	131	25	27	35	103	84	30	19	35
4	310	474	e100	123	24	26	42	103	126	32	19	36
5	291	598	e100	18	23	27	58	104	79	26	19	30
6	307	460	e98	18	24	27	73	98	38	26	19	27
7	281	347	e96	18	25	26	73	94	34	26	20	27
8	239	274	e94	18	25	27	83	100	47	26	23	26
9	231	252	e92	19	25	35	75	103	65	27	19	27
10	225	191	e90	19	25	26	54	108	86	26	26	27
11	1,410	188	e88	19	26	27	93	108	82	27	55	27
12	1,580	e190	e88	20	26	27	93	108	56	27	41	37
13	687	e190	e86	21	26	27	93	108	213	27	45	34
14	501	186	86	22	26	27	101	104	876	27	51	26
15	e420	171	84	21	26	27	108	95	554	27	54	31
16	341	e160	84	22	26	27	108	95	458	35	34	42
17	417	e160	84	22	26	40	103	95	601	28	25	52
18	532	e150	84	22	26	50	44	95	407	1,880	25	67
19	388	e150	84	22	26	37	47	95	314	1,680	26	75
20	334	143	82	22	26	27	50	95	178	757	26	75
21	291	142	69	22	26	35	52	95	114	394	26	75
22	265	e130	61	23	26	58	70	95	142	77	26	75
23	249	e130	56	23	27	66	79	99	33	20	26	75
24	1,510	e130	54	23	26	50	87	68	27	19	26	75
25	2,090	e130	47	23	27	55	90	55	35	19	26	53
26	913	e130	45	23	27	64	85	55	42	19	26	56
27	581	e120	44	23	26	42	87	41	57	19	26	43
28	444	e120	37	24	26	35	90	28	71	21	26	35
29	322	e120	31	24	26	35	90	30	71	20	26	27
30	e50	e120		24	26	51	90	33	73	20	26	27
31	35	e110		24		57		27	72		26	
Total	15,759	6,046	2,294	944	768	1,138	2,219	2,638	5,089	5,433	870	1,307
Mean	508	195	79.1	30.5	25.6	36.7	74.0	85.1	164	181	28.1	43.6

Year total 44,505 (ft³/s)-d

Mean 122 ft³/s

50

Table 14. Daily mean discharge, Wallenpaupack Creek at Wilsonville, Pennsylvania (station number 01432000), for report year ending November 30, 2004. (Record furnished by PPL Corporation)

[All values except total are in cubic feet per second, ft³/s; total in cubic feet per second days, (ft³/s)-d]

DAY	DEC	JAN	FEB	MAR	APR	MAY	JUNE	JULY	AUG	SEPT	OCT	NOV
1	596	1,060	0	100	347	0	345	184	416	570	858	337
2	796	1,060	350	128	338	0	264	147	578	599	906	310
3	713	1,020	320	75	0	272	314	0	580	613	906	230
4	897	831	391	95	0	690	296	0	441	377	821	314
5	903	1,020	342	170	998	1,020	0	0	308	284	821	317
6	1,060	1,030	340	2.0	1,020	960	0	338	402	299	826	0
7	945	908	0	0	465	1,010	333	453	0	489	827	0
8	986	985	0	417	449	0	440	280	0	602	907	286
9	984	977	378	358	505	0	611	382	402	748	903	293
10	678	1,100	432	341	14	676	474	0	445	973	906	315
11	1,160	900	339	373	0	889	430	0	528	922	829	296
12	1,680	860	336	281	315	952	0	242	790	929	908	516
13	1,720	800	335	46	356	975	0	383	1,030	935	896	0
14	1,720	715	0	0	425	1,060	377	349	1,620	896	908	0
15	1,700	444	0	303	355	8.0	280	290	1,620	858	829	201
16	1,670	714	353	304	278	158	293	526	1,570	946	832	527
17	1,720	877	344	278	0	955	382	0	1,420	1,050	832	399
18	1,730	826	301	249	0	910	348	0	1,570	794	530	569
19	1,090	780	353	291	106	965	0	288	1,570	1,590	493	297
20	1,090	714	339	0	158	1,040	0	268	1,390	1,580	529	0
21	1,040	762	0	0	191	966	277	275	500	1,560	436	0
22	1,060	634	0	410	169	27	262	327	438	1,560	587	369
23	1,100	711	106	421	173	0	325	328	451	1,560	637	261
24	1,410	915	82	301	0	840	347	352	550	1,560	722	309
25	1,670	714	70	711	0	769	294	396	534	864	970	0
26	1,030	680	105	413	0	577	0	487	393	857	1,070	0
27	1,050	475	64	0	0	501	0	797	602	827	654	0
28	1,050	710	0	0	0	270	177	815	479	896	405	0
29	1,070	516	0	327	0	0	229	782	515	774	631	775
30	1,060	547		393	0	0	231	996	635	903	4.0	1,070
31	1,040	22		240		0		505	602		0	
Total	36,418	24,307	5,680	7,027	6,662	16,490	7,329	10,190	22,379	27,415	22,383	7,991
Mean	1,175	784	196	227	222	532	244	329	722	914	722	266

Year total 194,271 (ft³/s)-d

Mean 531 ft³/s

51

Table 15. Daily mean discharge, Delaware River at Montague, New Jersey (station number 01438500), for report year ending November 30, 2004. (U.S. Geological Survey published record)

[All values except total are in cubic feet per second, ft³/s; total in cubic feet per second days, (ft³/s)-d; e, estimated]

DAY	DEC	JAN	FEB	MAR	APR	MAY	JUNE	JULY	AUG	SEPT	OCT	NOV
1	16,000	12,100	e3,000	2,000	8,030	7,420	4,770	1,840	5,040	8,820	15,800	3,700
2	13,700	11,100	e2,750	2,530	9,860	6,640	5,480	1,720	5,570	6,560	12,800	3,720
3	12,000	10,200	e2,900	4,330	9,450	8,320	5,640	1,610	5,110	5,130	11,500	3,850
4	10,800	11,400	e3,100	7,760	8,270	10,800	5,540	1,720	4,280	4,240	10,200	3,690
5	9,930	18,100	e2,900	10,200	7,990	9,170	4,790	1,770	3,780	3,350	8,910	4,570
6	9,480	19,000	e2,850	12,200	7,750	8,940	4,230	1,810	3,990	2,920	7,890	4,660
7	9,000	15,300	e3,150	19,400	6,880	8,820	4,420	2,170	3,620	2,820	6,970	3,740
8	7,950	12,700	e2,900	17,400	6,200	7,880	4,230	2,340	2,520	3,180	6,780	3,410
9	7,130	e10,500	e2,700	14,600	6,080	6,790	3,950	2,230	2,220	7,110	5,940	3,660
10	6,790	e7,500	e2,850	12,200	5,610	6,940	3,870	2,080	2,470	14,200	5,160	3,390
11	15,200	e6,100	e3,000	10,600	4,700	7,960	3,290	1,870	2,550	11,800	4,570	3,100
12	43,600	e7,250	e2,900	9,710	4,200	9,110	3,040	1,730	2,890	8,780	4,310	3,160
13	29,400	e7,850	e2,900	8,590	5,450	9,880	2,260	2,010	32,200	6,980	4,110	3,300
14	21,600	e7,200	e2,900	7,300	9,400	9,720	2,050	2,170	28,900	5,940	3,900	2,920
15	18,300	e5,650	e2,450	6,740	11,100	8,100	2,210	2,390	16,300	5,290	3,790	2,790
16	15,800	e4,500	e2,150	7,060	9,510	6,850	2,080	3,400	13,600	4,730	4,310	3,000
17	14,100	e5,000	e2,350	6,430	8,290	6,900	2,150	3,300	15,200	4,700	5,800	3,310
18	16,400	e5,450	e2,600	5,970	7,050	6,510	2,700	2,540	13,000	81,700	4,710	3,170
19	15,000	e5,450	e2,500	5,620	6,470	6,360	2,750	2,660	10,500	116,000	5,010	3,230
20	12,900	e5,200	e2,500	5,260	6,180	5,910	2,300	3,510	9,140	49,200	11,000	3,010
21	11,800	e4,600	e2,700	5,160	5,870	5,170	1,760	3,070	8,690	31,000	8,590	2,800
22	10,400	e4,350	2,430	6,040	5,450	4,470	1,910	2,750	10,300	22,100	6,950	2,920
23	9,790	e3,900	2,230	5,780	5,450	3,650	1,840	2,680	8,710	16,800	6,510	3,400
24	14,000	e3,550	2,490	5,250	6,430	3,750	1,820	4,510	6,710	13,900	5,820	3,280
25	38,600	e3,350	2,410	5,580	5,960	4,350	1,790	4,430	5,700	12,300	5,640	3,870
26	32,000	e3,350	2,190	6,050	6,060	3,950	1,740	3,360	5,280	9,850	5,450	6,150
27	24,000	e3,250	2,140	6,330	11,600	4,660	1,730	3,010	4,790	e7,650	5,170	6,260
28	19,100	e3,200	2,060	8,130	10,700	6,140	1,930	10,700	4,490	e10,500	4,520	10,900
29	15,900	e3,350	1,870	8,730	9,160	6,300	1,780	11,800	3,980	20,100	4,420	33,300
30	14,000	e3,300		8,390	8,290	5,770	1,700	9,780	4,420	18,500	4,140	21,300
31	13,200	e3,250		8,010		4,860		6,350	8,020		3,860	
Total	507,870	227,000	75,870	249,350	223,440	212,090	89,750	107,310	253,970	516,150	204,530	163,560
Mean	16,380	7,323	2,616	8,044	7,448	6,842	2,992	3,462	8,193	17,200	6,598	5,452

Year total 2,830,890 (ft³/s)-d

Mean 7,735 ft³/s

Table 16. Diversions by New Jersey; daily mean discharge, Delaware and Raritan Canal at Port Mercer, New Jersey (station number 01460440), for report year ending November 30, 2004.

(U.S. Geological Survey published record)

[All data except total are in million gallons per day, Mgal/d; total in Million gallons, Mgal; e, estimated]

DAY	DEC	JAN	FEB	MAR	APR	MAY	JUNE	JULY	AUG	SEPT	OCT	NOV
1	85	84	e86	95	89	92	91	e81	94	93	92	87
2	90	81	e85	97	90	93	91	e79	94	93	88	89
3	91	80	e90	94	85	90	94	e87	90	93	93	88
4	91	80	e95	96	88	89	92	80	97	93	94	84
5	92	85	96	95	89	90	93	95	95	93	95	73
6	94	91	40	95	91	91	92	93	93	94	88	81
7	91	90	30	93	94	92	93	94	94	94	88	85
8	90	89	83	88	93	93	93	92	95	96	e84	85
9	90	88	94	84	93	93	92	90	95	94	e81	85
10	91	92	97	91	93	94	90	93	95	93	e78	87
11	-51	99	94	93	92	94	90	95	95	93	e72	85
12	50	99	98	92	94	94	91	85	76	93	e70	87
13	84	98	97	91	67	92	92	79	89	93	e68	74
14	55	96	91	91	42	91	93	90	92	93	e65	78
15	-30	98	91	93	70	91	94	90	91	96	e87	81
16	80	99	89	94	84	93	94	91	94	95	e97	83
17	76	102	91	95	86	88	93	94	93	95	91	84
18	81	101	92	93	91	91	93	94	97	98	89	85
19	85	98	90	89	91	91	92	94	97	90	87	86
20	87	98	91	85	92	84	90	93	97	88	84	87
21	88	99	91	83	90	77	93	93	98	60	84	86
22	88	100	91	86	91	92	e94	93	95	95	82	86
23	87	101	91	86	94	88	e90	87	95	99	82	86
24	41	102	92	90	91	e74	e92	89	96	99	87	88
25	69	103	92	93	88	e90	e92	95	95	97	90	87
26	82	103	91	94	86	e94	86	95	96	95	88	83
27	87	102	93	94	73	95	e85	94	94	92	88	84
28	89	103	92	95	84	96	e85	66	95	77	89	61
29	88	93	92	94	88	91	e84	91	93	-24	87	75
30	89	e90		92	91	92	e83	94	95	83	89	81
31	88	e88		91		93		95	95		87	
Total	2,318	2,932	2,545	2,842	2,590	2,808	2,727	2,781	2,910	2,643	2,644	2,491
Mean	74.8	94.6	87.8	91.7	86.3	90.6	90.9	89.7	93.9	88.1	85.3	83.0

Year total 32,231 Mgal

Mean 88.1 Mgal/d

QUALITY OF WATER IN THE DELAWARE ESTUARY

Introduction

This section describes the water-quality monitoring program for the Delaware Estuary during the River Master 2004 report year, December 1, 2003, to November 30, 2004. This program is conducted by the USGS, in cooperation with the Delaware River Basin Commission (DRBC). Selected data collected for this program are presented and water-quality conditions are summarized. The DRBC and others use these data to assess water-quality conditions and track the movement of the "salt front" in the Delaware Estuary.

Water-Quality Monitoring Program

As part of a long-term program, the quality of water in the Delaware Estuary between Trenton, New Jersey, and Reedy Island Jetty, Delaware, is monitored at various locations (fig. 6). Data on water temperature, specific conductance, dissolved oxygen, and pH were collected by electronic instruments at four sites—Trenton, Benjamin Franklin Bridge (Philadelphia), Chester, and Reedy Island Jetty. Water-quality monitors at Trenton and Reedy Island Jetty were operated continuously throughout the report year, whereas monitors at the Benjamin Franklin Bridge and Chester were operated from April to November 2004.

Water-quality data were collected on a monthly basis in March, June, July, and October, and on a semi-monthly basis in April, May, August, and September 2004 at 19 sites between Biles Channel and Mahon River (sample sites A–T on fig. 6). These data were collected by the State of Delaware for the DRBC. At each of these sites, water samples were collected at a single point near the center of the channel and analyzed for selected physical properties and chemical constituents including temperature, chloride, alkalinity, specific conductance, dissolved oxygen, pH, nutrients, and trace metals. These analyses consist of field measurements and laboratory determinations.

From March to October, water-quality data were obtained on a monthly basis at three additional sites in the lower Delaware Bay (sites U–W on fig. 6). Water samples were analyzed for selected physical properties and chemical constituents.

Data obtained from the water-quality monitors are processed and stored in the USGS National Water Information System data base. These data are published annually by the USGS in water resources data reports for New Jersey and Pennsylvania. Water-quality data for the other sampling sites are not presented in this report but are available from DRBC and STORET, an environmental quality database operated by the U.S. Environmental Protection Agency.

Water Quality During the 2004 Report Year

Streamflow

Streamflow has a major effect on the quality of water in the Delaware Estuary. High freshwater flows commonly result in improved water quality by limiting the upstream movement of seawater and reducing the concentration of dissolved substances. High flows also aid in maintaining lower water temperatures during warm weather and in supporting higher concentrations of dissolved oxygen. Under certain conditions, however, high streamflows can transport large quantities of nutrients to the estuary, which may result in algal blooms.

Streamflow from the Delaware River Basin above Trenton, New Jersey, is the major source of freshwater inflow to the Delaware Estuary. During the report year, monthly mean streamflow recorded at the USGS gaging station Delaware River at Trenton, New Jersey, was highest during December 2003 (35,510 ft^3/s) and lowest during June 2004 (7,050 ft^3/s; table 17). Monthly mean streamflows were less than long-

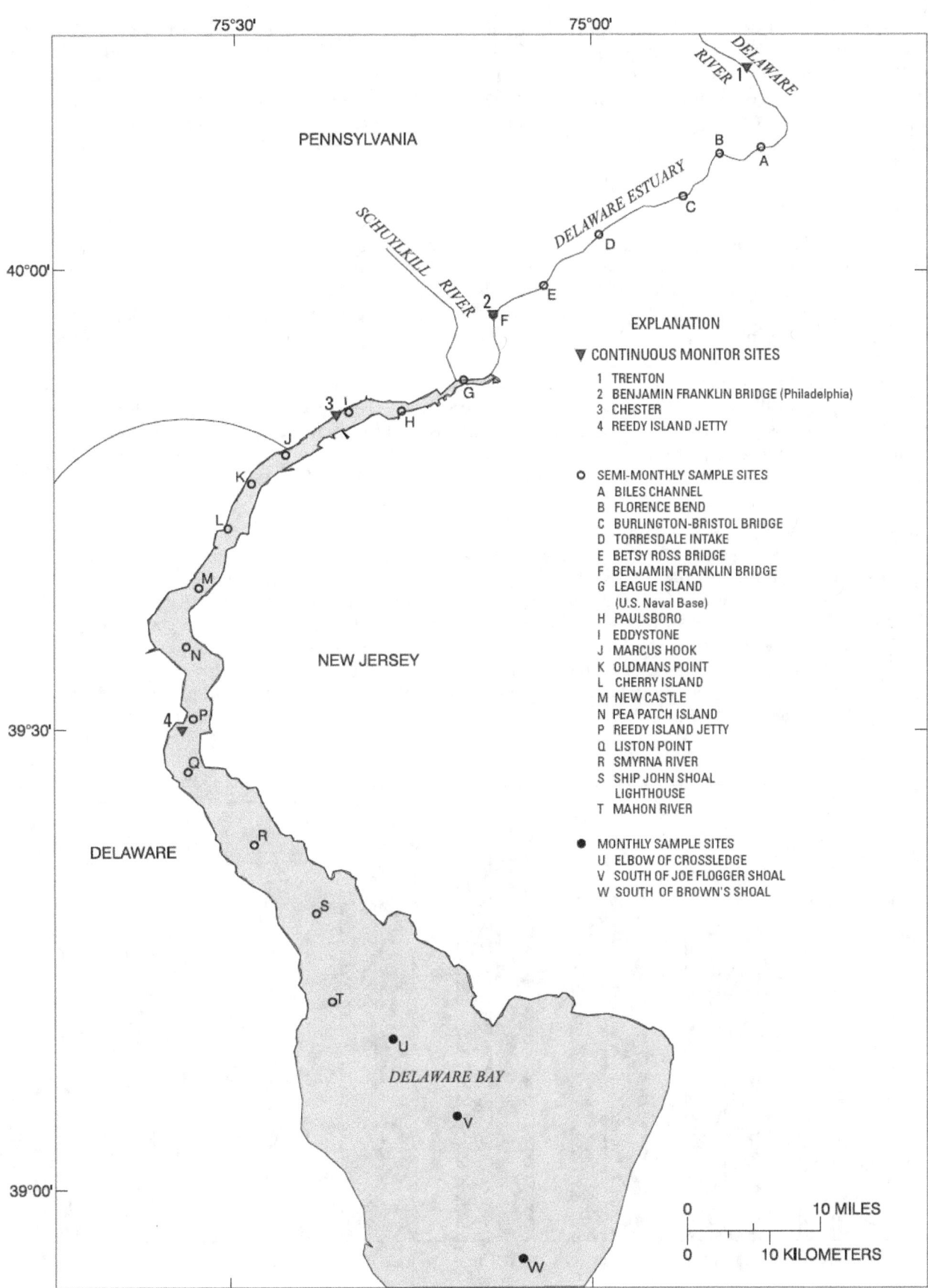

Figure 6. Location of water-quality monitoring sites on the Delaware Estuary.

term mean monthly flows in February, March, April, and June and greater than the long-term flows in the other 8 months. The greatest percentage flow deficiency was in February 2004, when monthly mean streamflow was 68 percent of the long-term mean monthly flow. Long-term mean monthly streamflow was computed on the basis of data for the period from 1913 to 2003. The highest daily mean streamflow during the report year was 181,000 ft³/s on September 19, 2004. The lowest daily mean streamflow was 3,590 ft³/s on July 7, 2004.

Water Temperature

Water temperature has an important influence on water quality, as it affects various physical, chemical, and biological properties of water. Generally, increases in water temperature have detrimental effects on water quality by decreasing the saturation level of dissolved oxygen and increasing the biological activity of aquatic organisms. Although the primary factors that affect water temperature in the Delaware Estuary are climatic, various kinds of water use, especially powerplant cooling, also can have significant effects.

Water temperature records for the monitor site at the Benjamin Franklin Bridge, Philadelphia, Pennsylvania show that monthly mean temperatures during the report year were greater than the long-term mean monthly temperatures in April, May, and June 2004 and were less than the long-term means for the period from July to November 2004. Long-term mean water temperatures were computed using data from 1964 to 2003 (fig. 7). The maximum daily mean water temperature of 26.7°C was recorded on July 11, 2004.

Specific Conductance and Chloride

Specific conductance is a measure of the capacity of water to conduct an electrical current and is a function of the types and quantities of dissolved substances in water. As concentrations of dissolved ions increase, specific conductance of the water increases. Specific conductance measurements are good indicators of dissolved solids content and total ion concentrations. Seawater and some man-made constituents can cause the specific conductance of estuary water to increase substantially. Dilution associated with high streamflows results in decreased levels of dissolved solids and lower specific conductance, whereas low streamflows have the opposite effect.

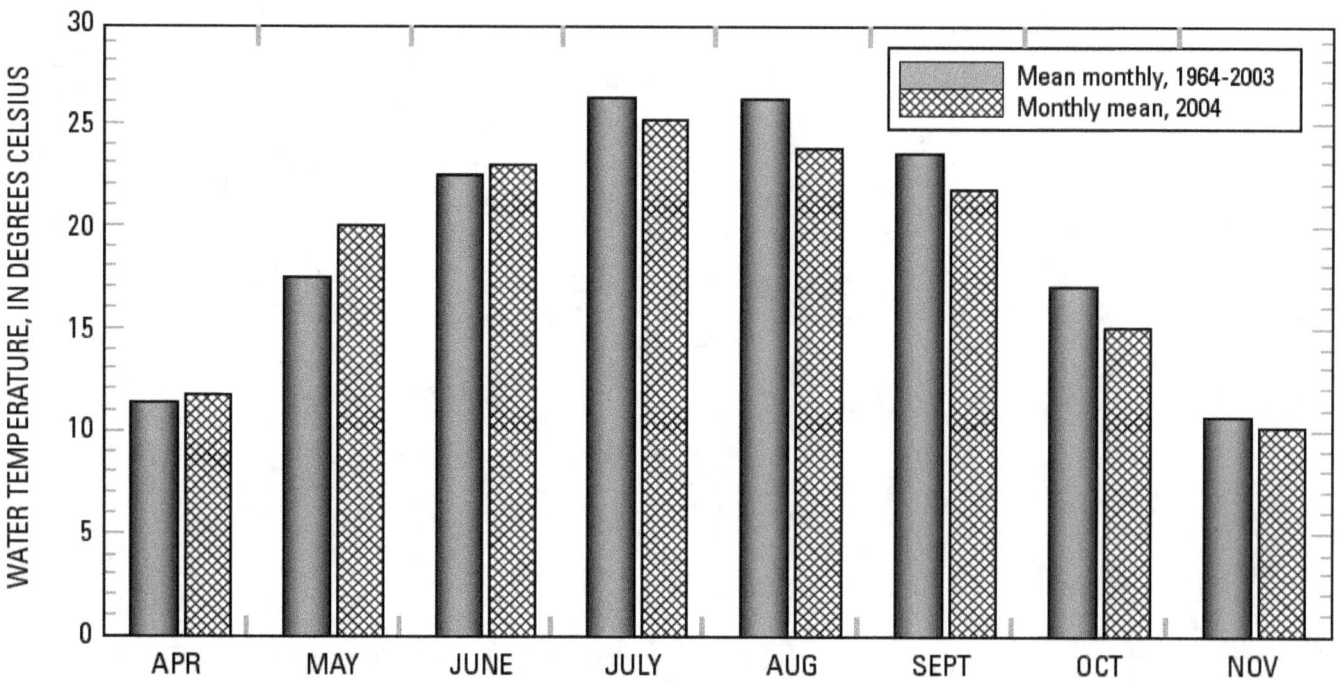

Figure 7. Water temperature in the Delaware Estuary at Benjamin Franklin Bridge at Philadelphia, Pennsylvania, April to November.

The upstream movement of seawater and the accompanying increase in chloride concentrations is an important concern for water supplies obtained from the Delaware Estuary. Water with chloride concentrations greater than 250 mg/L (milligrams per liter) is considered undesirable for domestic use, and water with concentrations exceeding 50 mg/L is unsatisfactory for some industrial processes. Chloride concentrations in the estuary increase in a downstream direction, with proximity to the Atlantic Ocean.

Chloride concentration was not measured directly at the monitor site at Reedy Island Jetty, Delaware. Instead, a mathematical relation between specific conductance and chloride concentration has been developed on the basis of long-term field measurements of specific conductance and laboratory analyses of chloride; this relation can be used to estimate chloride concentrations from specific conductance values. Chloride concentrations estimated from the relation are presented in table 18. The specific conductance-chloride relation is less reliable when chloride concentrations are less than 30 mg/L, because other dissolved ions may be present in amounts large enough to affect the relation. Therefore, chloride concentrations estimated from specific conductance data are not presented when concentrations of less than 30 mg/L would result from the relation. Instead, estimated values less than 30 mg/L are reported as < 30 mg/L. Chloride concentrations at Chester, Pa. (table 19), were measured directly by Kimberly Clark Chester Operations and are not derived from specific conductance data.

At Chester, the highest daily maximum chloride concentration was 82 mg/L on February 6, 2004 (table 19). During the report year, daily maximum concentrations exceeded 50 mg/L on nearly 15 percent of the days. The lowest daily minimum chloride concentration was 10 mg/L on September 30. Daily minimum concentrations exceeded 50 mg/L on nearly 8 percent of the days. Chloride concentrations were persistently high from January 29 to February 17, 2004, and from July 5–14 when daily minimum concentrations exceeded 50 mg/L on all days except January 31.

At Reedy Island Jetty, the highest daily maximum chloride concentration was 8,000 mg/L on February 3, 2004 (table 18). Daily maximum chloride concentrations during the report year exceeded 1,000 mg/L on 88 percent of the days. The lowest daily minimum chloride concentration for the report year was <30 mg/L on several days in each of the following months—December 2003, and January, September, and October 2004. Daily minimum chloride concentrations exceeded 1,000 mg/L on 37 percent of the days. From December to May, daily maximum chloride concentrations at Reedy Island Jetty ranged from <30 to 8,000 mg/L. From June to November, daily maximum chloride concentrations ranged from <30 to 5,400 mg/L.

Dissolved Oxygen

Dissolved oxygen in water is necessary for the respiratory processes of aquatic organisms and in chemical reactions in aquatic environments. Fish and many other clean-water species require relatively high dissolved-oxygen concentrations at all times. The major source of dissolved oxygen in the Delaware Estuary is diffusion from the atmosphere, and, to a lesser extent, photosynthetic activity of aquatic plants. The principal factors that affect dissolved oxygen concentrations in the Estuary are water temperature, biochemical oxygen demand, freshwater inflow, phytoplankton, turbidity, salinity, and tidal and wind-driven mixing.

Concentrations of dissolved oxygen at several sites on the Delaware Estuary have been measured since 1962 by the USGS. Two of these sites, Delaware River at Benjamin Franklin Bridge at Philadelphia, Pennsylvania, and Delaware River at Chester, Pennsylvania, have nearly continuous records and are in the reach of the estuary most affected by effluent discharges. For these stations, the mean and minimum daily mean dissolved oxygen concentrations for the 3-month period of July to September during each of the 1965–2004 report years is shown in figure 8. An increasing trend in concentration is evident. Although concentrations have increased considerably over this 40-year period, mean concentrations can vary substantially from year to year.

Concentrations of dissolved oxygen in the Delaware Estuary generally are greatest near Trenton and decrease in a downstream direction. In an area just below the Benjamin Franklin Bridge, concentrations

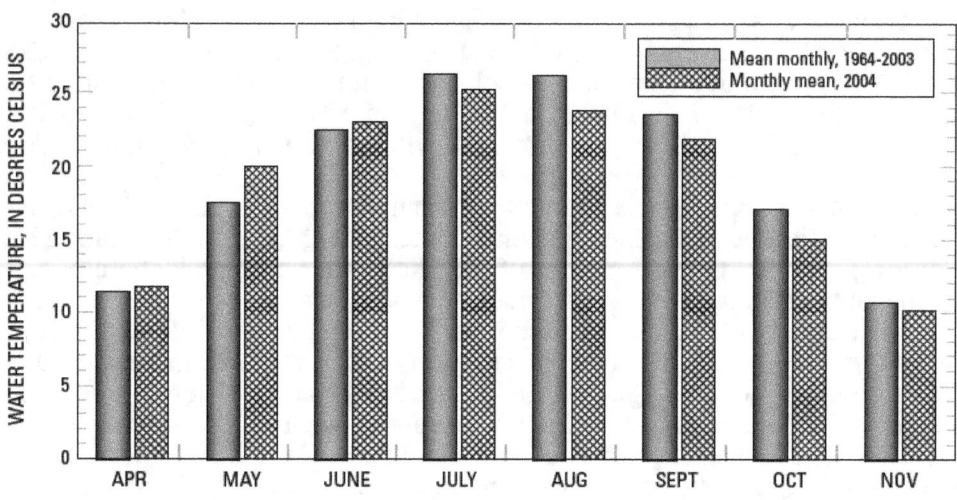

Figure 8. Mean and minimum daily mean dissolved oxygen concentrations from July to September at two monitor sites on the Delaware Estuary, 1965–2004.

usually reach minimum levels. During the report year, daily mean concentrations of dissolved oxygen at the Benjamin Franklin Bridge monitor site were lowest in late June and early July, and the lowest recorded daily mean concentration was 3.6 mg/L on June 29 (table 20). Daily mean concentrations of dissolved oxygen were consistently 6.0 mg/L or greater on most days from April 1 to June 1 and on all days from September 22 to November 27, 2004. At Chester, daily mean dissolved oxygen concentrations were lowest during late July and early August, and the lowest recorded daily mean concentration was 3.8 mg/L on August 5 (table 21).

Histograms of hourly dissolved oxygen concentrations at the Benjamin Franklin Bridge and Chester monitor sites during the critical summer period—July to September 2004—are presented in figure 9. Hourly concentrations at the Benjamin Franklin Bridge were 4 mg/L or less during 13 percent of this period. At Chester, hourly dissolved oxygen concentrations were 4 mg/L or less during 14 percent of the 2004 critical summer period. Dissolved oxygen concentrations less than 4 mg/L can have adverse, and possibly lethal, effects on fish and other aquatic organisms.

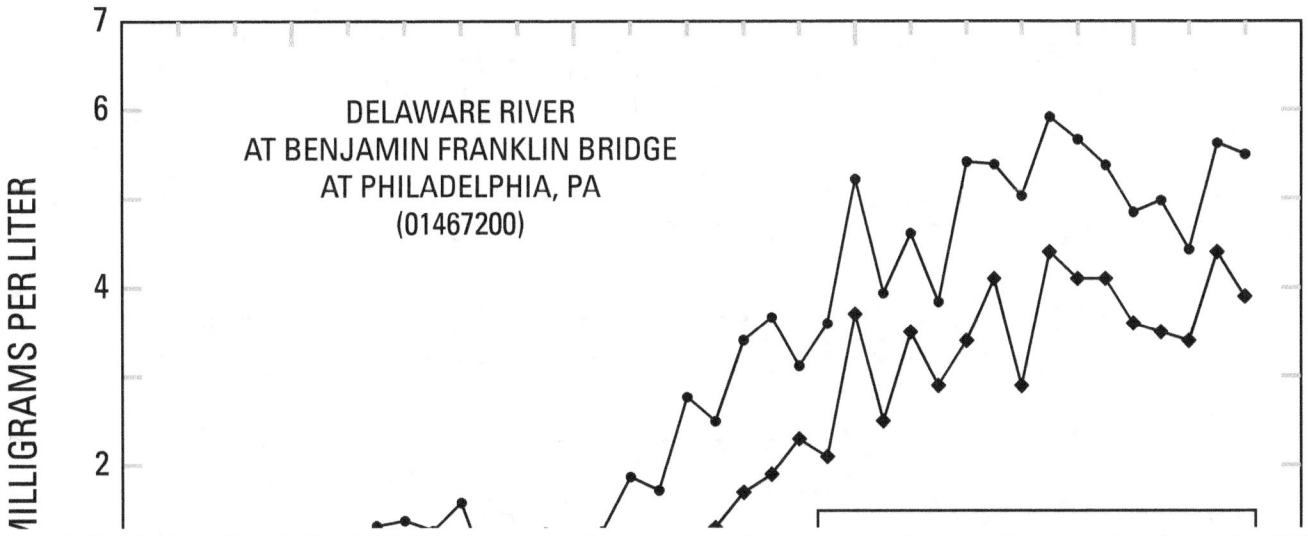

Figure 9. Distribution of hourly dissolved oxygen concentrations at two monitor sites on the Delaware Estuary, July to September 2004.

Hydrogen-Ion Activity (pH)

The pH of a solution is a measure of the effective concentration (activity) of dissolved hydrogen ions. Solutions having pH less than 7 are characterized as acidic, whereas solutions with pH greater than 7 are considered basic or alkaline. The pH of uncontaminated surface water generally ranges from 6.5 to 8.5. Major factors affecting the pH of surface water include the geologic composition of the drainage basin and human inputs, including wastewater discharges. In addition, photosynthetic activity, and dissolved gases including carbon dioxide, hydrogen sulfide, and ammonia can have a considerable effect on pH. During the report year, pH was measured seasonally at the Benjamin Franklin Bridge and Chester monitor sites, and continuously at the Reedy Island Jetty site. The range of daily median pH for these stations is as follows: Benjamin Franklin Bridge, 6.6 to 7.7; Chester, 6.8 to 7.6; and Reedy Island Jetty, 6.9 to 7.8. Generally, the pH of water in the Delaware Estuary is lowest near Trenton, New Jersey, and increases (that is, becomes more alkaline) in a downstream direction. The pH of water in the Delaware Estuary between the Benjamin Franklin Bridge and Reedy Island Jetty is not a limiting factor for aquatic health and other beneficial uses of the water.

Table 17. Daily mean discharge, Delaware River at Trenton, New Jersey (station number 01463500), for report year ending November 30, 2004. (U.S. Geological Survey published record)

[All values, except total, are in cubic feet per second ft³/s; total in cubic feet per second days, (ft³/s)-d; e, estimated]

DAY	DEC	JAN	FEB	MAR	APR	MAY	JUNE	JULY	AUG	SEPT	OCT	NOV
1	35,900	25,700	e7,100	6,710	15,800	15,300	11,000	4,240	14,500	14,100	39,700	9,020
2	31,800	23,400	e7,000	7,130	15,900	14,300	10,600	3,980	12,100	13,900	31,800	e8,550
3	28,200	21,600	e7,000	8,260	17,800	14,400	10,900	4,010	11,500	11,800	26,000	8,410
4	24,600	20,300	e8,100	10,800	17,100	20,000	10,600	3,780	11,200	10,000	23,300	8,530
5	21,900	25,400	e8,500	16,500	15,500	21,400	10,200	3,630	10,100	8,610	20,200	9,960
6	20,400	35,700	e10,400	20,000	14,400	18,500	9,730	3,600	8,630	7,560	17,500	10,100
7	19,000	33,500	e20,000	24,300	13,600	17,600	9,580	3,590	7,860	6,550	16,000	10,300
8	17,900	27,800	e16,000	31,600	13,000	17,800	9,020	3,660	7,370	6,380	14,600	8,880
9	16,500	23,500	11,900	29,000	12,200	16,400	8,730	3,980	6,250	13,500	14,100	8,120
10	15,300	19,800	10,300	24,500	11,800	14,800	7,910	4,000	5,240	20,500	13,100	8,130
11	40,900	15,700	10,400	21,000	11,100	14,700	8,110	3,810	5,010	25,400	12,000	7,740
12	66,800	14,600	9,830	18,700	9,960	17,800	8,000	4,520	5,540	20,900	10,700	7,710
13	71,300	16,000	8,890	16,900	14,800	18,700	7,040	14,200	10,800	16,600	10,100	10,400
14	54,700	16,300	8,590	15,600	21,800	19,400	6,260	9,600	52,900	13,900	9,640	9,680
15	48,700	15,100	8,210	14,000	26,400	18,300	5,520	11,700	39,600	11,700	9,640	8,300
16	37,800	13,800	7,490	13,200	24,100	17,900	5,280	8,020	26,500	10,700	10,900	7,840
17	36,500	e13,400	6,530	13,700	20,100	15,700	5,420	7,160	22,300	9,950	11,500	7,700
18	38,900	e12,000	6,510	13,000	17,400	14,600	5,440	7,450	22,100	42,700	12,000	7,930
19	35,300	e12,400	6,870	12,900	15,700	13,600	6,370	8,140	18,900	181,000	11,800	7,800
20	30,900	12,600	6,910	13,200	14,300	13,400	6,370	8,500	15,800	139,000	13,400	7,730
21	27,000	12,600	6,940	14,600	13,400	12,500	5,830	7,830	17,600	72,300	18,200	7,740
22	24,400	11,700	7,570	14,000	12,800	11,300	5,180	7,240	32,300	50,800	16,500	7,510
23	21,900	e10,400	7,690	13,900	12,200	10,400	4,980	6,940	25,600	38,900	14,500	7,230
24	29,700	e9,000	7,100	13,300	11,900	9,020	5,220	8,140	20,400	31,100	13,300	7,470
25	52,000	e8,100	7,140	12,500	12,600	8,420	4,770	8,060	16,600	25,800	12,300	8,770
26	65,300	e8,000	6,800	12,500	13,800	8,770	4,990	8,290	14,200	22,000	11,600	10,900
27	50,800	e7,900	6,500	13,200	19,600	9,300	4,860	7,640	12,500	18,300	11,000	12,100
28	40,600	e7,800	6,420	13,600	22,000	13,200	4,610	23,400	11,200	22,100	10,700	27,000
29	34,200	e7,500	6,600	15,000	19,500	14,100	4,440	20,000	10,900	61,600	9,720	55,700
30	32,000	e7,600		15,500	16,800	13,000	4,530	19,100	9,800	49,400	9,580	55,800
31	29,600	e7,500		15,900		12,000		15,700	11,100		9,870	
Total	1,100,800	496,100	249,290	485,000	477,360	456,610	211,490	235,910	496,400	977,050	465,250	373,050
Mean	35,510	16,020	8,596	15,650	15,910	14,730	7,050	8,191	16,010	32,570	15,010	12,440

Year total 6,042,910 (ft³/s)-d

Mean 16,510 ft³/s

Table 18. Daily maximum and minimum chloride concentrations estimated from values of specific conductance, Delaware River at Reedy Island Jetty, Delaware (station number 01482800), for report year ending November 30, 2004.

[Concentrations in milligrams per liter; ---, missing data; Max, maximum value; Min, minimum value; <, less than; n.d., not determined]

DAY	DEC Max	DEC Min	JAN Max	JAN Min	FEB Max	FEB Min	MAR Max	MAR Min	APR Max	APR Min	MAY Max	MAY Min	JUNE Max	JUNE Min	JULY Max	JULY Min	AUG Max	AUG Min	SEPT Max	SEPT Min	OCT Max	OCT Min	NOV Max	NOV Min
1	84	<30	220	<30	6,100	2,900	5,500	2,400	3,600	1,400	2,900	580	5,000	1,300	5,200	1,800	1,800	390	1,500	220	<30	<30	2,700	960
2	550	<30	910	<30	7,100	3,300	5,900	2,500	3,400	1,400	2,800	670	5,000	1,500	5,100	1,900	880	290	1,100	230	<30	<30	3,300	990
3	2,000	<30	1,400	<30	8,000	4,300	6,100	2,400	3,500	1,300	2,800	560	4,500	1,300	5,000	1,900	910	260	1,500	250	<30	<30	3,200	1,000
4	2,300	260	1,400	42	7,200	2,900	6,500	2,500	3,100	1,000	2,300	410	4,400	1,400	5,300	2,000	1,200	240	920	240	330	<30	3,700	1,200
5	3,100	360	1,700	110	6,200	2,400	6,500	2,700	2,000	720	2,300	400	4,500	1,400	5,000	2,100	920	240	2,300	260	670	<30	3,500	1,400
6	3,400	920	1,400	94	6,300	2,200	5,900	2,800	2,900	660	---	---	4,400	1,400	4,600	2,100	1,900	250	2,000	530	1,600	44	3,200	840
7	4,000	830	810	46	4,900	1,500	4,900	2,100	4,300	820	---	---	4,500	1,400	4,600	2,100	2,700	270	2,000	480	1,900	210	3,800	820
8	4,300	1,200	800	30	2,800	810	4,000	1,800	4,100	1,000	---	---	3,900	1,500	4,200	2,300	2,500	290	2,600	480	2,400	350	4,300	1,500
9	4,600	1,200	1,900	<30	2,500	640	5,000	1,500	4,200	1,200	---	---	3,600	1,500	4,200	2,200	3,100	380	2,700	1,000	3,200	710	4,300	1,400
10	4,100	1,500	2,100	120	2,800	630	4,300	1,600	3,500	1,000	---	---	3,300	1,400	4,700	2,100	3,700	530	2,200	360	3,000	790	5,400	1,700
11	4,200	680	2,400	170	3,000	590	4,800	1,400	3,200	960	---	310	3,900	1,400	4,800	2,000	4,300	910	2,600	400	4,300	840	5,000	1,900
12	1,100	220	1,600	220	2,900	560	4,800	1,400	3,100	990	1,000	310	4,000	1,500	---	---	4,300	840	2,900	490	4,300	1,400	4,600	1,700
13	640	190	2,100	240	3,100	590	2,500	850	3,600	1,000	1,300	260	3,900	1,600	---	---	4,200	1,000	2,900	480	4,900	1,600	5,300	2,000
14	2,300	130	1,700	200	2,900	520	2,900	800	2,700	840	1,400	270	3,400	1,500	3,200	1,400	3,600	630	2,700	500	3,900	1,700	5,300	1,800
15	390	38	2,000	330	3,200	490	3,400	900	2,400	500	1,200	230	3,300	1,100	3,200	1,000	2,500	400	2,800	590	4,700	1,700	5,200	1,800
16	710	44	700	190	3,400	620	3,400	920	2,700	400	1,400	190	3,100	990	3,200	860	2,300	320	2,100	610	4,100	1,500	5,000	1,700
17	900	110	2,900	190	3,600	850	4,300	1,200	2,700	430	1,400	190	3,200	1,000	---	---	2,400	310	2,300	620	3,000	910	5,000	1,700
18	990	40	4,100	540	4,000	1,000	4,400	1,200	1,000	360	---	---	3,400	1,000	---	---	2,000	340	2,400	560	3,100	850	4,800	1,600
19	670	42	4,200	850	5,300	1,300	3,900	1,200	1,400	340	---	---	3,500	1,100	---	---	1,400	290	1,500	56	3,000	920	4,600	1,800
20	1,500	33	3,400	630	5,200	1,500	3,900	940	1,300	270	---	---	3,900	1,100	3,200	1,000	1,200	280	120	<30	4,100	1,000	4,800	1,700
21	1,300	33	3,400	560	4,400	1,600	3,200	970	1,600	320	---	---	4,300	1,300	---	---	1,000	280	110	35	3,700	1,300	4,500	1,900
22	260	38	5,000	810	3,300	1,400	2,300	780	1,500	300	---	---	4,100	1,200	---	---	1,500	230	630	45	3,700	1,300	4,100	1,800
23	820	36	3,700	740	4,000	1,400	3,000	720	1,300	320	1,800	270	4,000	1,100	3,200	860	1,200	150	930	58	3,600	1,400	4,200	2,000
24	950	37	4,600	1,000	3,700	1,400	2,300	640	1,300	310	2,100	300	4,100	1,300	2,700	940	1,200	130	1,800	47	3,900	1,400	4,600	2,000
25	370	38	3,500	1,200	3,200	1,500	1,900	630	1,300	320	2,300	340	4,000	1,400	3,900	940	1,600	150	1,400	160	3,700	1,400	4,800	1,700
26	51	<30	4,300	1,400	4,400	1,600	2,100	570	1,700	330	3,000	690	3,800	1,600	4,100	1,200	1,800	160	1,500	150	3,700	1,300	3,400	1,400
27	34	<30	5,300	2,200	3,900	1,600	1,700	510	1,300	340	3,400	790	4,400	1,500	3,600	1,300	1,700	190	1,500	170	3,500	1,300	4,200	1,500
28	<30	<30	4,600	2,100	4,800	1,800	1,900	510	1,600	260	3,600	1,100	4,700	1,500	2,900	770	1,700	190	1,800	220	3,400	1,200	4,600	1,200
29	<30	<30	4,400	1,900	5,500	2,200	2,800	890	2,800	440	3,700	920	5,000	1,600	2,900	550	1,500	220	500	<30	3,400	1,200	2,300	710
30	<30	<30	5,000	2,300			2,600	1,200	2,800	520	4,200	1,000	5,200	1,700	2,900	470	1,400	220	150	<30	3,300	1,200	1,800	400
31	81	<30	5,600	2,000			2,900	990			4,300	1,200			2,400	480	1,700	230			3,200	1,000		
Mean	n.d.	n.d.	n.d.	n.d.	4,400	1,500	3,900	1,300	2,500	670	2,500	500	4,100	1,400	4,000	1,400	2,000	340	1,700	n.d.	n.d.	n.d.	4,200	1,500
Max	4,600	1,500	5,600	2,300	8,000	4,300	6,500	2,800	4,300	1,400	4,300	1,200	5,200	1,700	5,300	2,300	4,300	1,000	2,900	1,000	4,900	1,700	5,400	2,000
Min	<30	<30	220	<30	2,500	490	1,700	510	1,000	260	1,000	190	3,100	990	2,400	470	880	130	110	<30	<30	<30	1,800	400

61

Table 19. Daily maximum and minimum chloride concentrations, Delaware River at Chester, Pennsylvania (station number 01477050), for report year ending November 30, 2004.

(Record furnished by Kimberly Clark Chester Operations)

[Concentrations in milligrams per liter; --, missing data; Max, maximum value; Min, minimum value]

DAY	DEC Max	DEC Min	JAN Max	JAN Min	FEB Max	FEB Min	MAR Max	MAR Min	APR Max	APR Min	MAY Max	MAY Min	JUNE Max	JUNE Min	JULY Max	JULY Min	AUG Max	AUG Min	SEPT Max	SEPT Min	OCT Max	OCT Min	NOV Max	NOV Min
1	25	25	31	31	51	51	57	50	49	49	37	37	37	31	43	37	38	26	37	31	31	31	33	31
2	25	25	31	31	51	51	43	43	49	42	37	37	37	31	43	37	37	31	31	25	31	31	31	31
3	25	25	31	31	58	51	50	43	49	42	43	43	37	31	43	37	37	37	31	31	30	30	33	33
4	31	25	31	31	74	51	43	43	42	42	37	31	37	31	51	43	31	31	31	25	25	25	39	39
5	31	31	31	25	65	57	50	43	42	42	37	31	37	31	53	51	37	31	31	25	25	19	39	33
6	31	25	31	31	82	65	50	43	42	42	37	31	37	37	51	51	31	31	31	31	25	13	39	33
7	28	25	31	31	73	57	43	43	42	36	37	37	43	31	58	51	31	31	27	27	25	19	39	33
8	37	26	31	31	73	65	43	43	49	42	37	37	37	37	66	51	31	31	31	25	--	--	39	39
9	44	37	31	31	65	57	50	43	42	42	37	37	37	37	74	51	31	31	31	25	--	--	39	39
10	44	43	31	25	57	57	50	43	42	42	37	37	31	31	66	51	31	31	31	31	--	--	39	33
11	58	50	31	25	65	57	50	35	42	36	37	37	43	37	61	58	31	31	37	37	--	--	39	33
12	66	43	31	25	65	57	43	43	42	36	37	37	37	37	67	58	31	31	31	31	25	25	39	33
13	37	31	37	31	73	57	43	43	42	42	37	37	37	37	51	51	31	25	31	31	31	31	36	36
14	37	31	51	25	65	57	37	37	42	36	37	31	37	37	51	51	37	31	31	25	31	25	39	33
15	43	37	51	25	57	57	43	43	42	36	31	31	31	31	51	44	37	31	31	31	27	25	33	31
16	43	31	31	31	57	57	43	43	42	36	37	31	37	37	51	37	37	25	31	31	31	27	39	33
17	43	31	31	31	57	57	50	37	36	36	37	31	37	37	37	31	31	31	31	31	27	25	33	31
18	43	37	37	31	50	50	50	37	42	36	37	37	37	31	44	31	31	31	31	31	31	27	39	33
19	37	37	51	37	57	50	43	43	36	36	37	31	43	37	60	31	31	31	32	29	31	25	39	36
20	37	37	51	31	57	50	50	50	42	38	37	31	37	37	37	37	37	31	31	31	31	25	39	39
21	37	37	51	37	57	50	50	43	37	37	37	31	37	37	37	37	31	25	31	31	31	31	39	39
22	37	31	51	31	57	50	43	43	37	31	37	31	37	37	37	37	31	25	31	31	27	25	33	33
23	37	31	51	37	50	43	50	43	37	31	37	37	43	31	37	37	31	25	25	25	31	27	39	33
24	37	31	37	37	57	50	50	43	43	37	37	31	37	37	37	31	37	31	31	31	31	25	39	33
25	37	31	51	44	57	50	50	50	37	31	37	31	37	37	37	37	37	31	31	31	31	25	39	33
26	31	31	51	31	50	43	50	43	37	31	31	31	43	37	37	31	37	25	31	31	31	31	33	33
27	31	31	51	44	50	50	50	43	43	37	37	31	37	37	37	31	31	25	31	31	31	31	39	39
28	31	31	51	44	50	43	50	43	43	31	37	31	37	31	37	37	31	25	31	31	31	31	39	39
29	31	31	51	51	57	43	50	42	43	37	37	31	41	31	37	27	37	27	31	31	31	31	39	39
30	31	31	51	51			42	42	43	37	37	31	37	37	37	20	37	25	10	10	25	25	39	39
31	31	31	51	44			42	42			31	31			34	27	37	25			33	33		
Mean	37	32	39	33	60	53	47	43	42	38	36	34	38	35	47	40	34	29	30	29	29	28	38	35
Max	66	50	51	51	82	65	57	50	49	49	43	43	43	37	74	58	38	37	37	37	33	33	39	39
Min	25	25	31	25	50	43	37	35	36	31	31	31	31	31	34	20	31	25	10	10	25	13	31	31

Table 20. Daily mean dissolved oxygen concentration, Delaware River at Benjamin Franklin Bridge at Philadelphia, Pennsylvania (station number 01467200), April 1 to November 30, 2004.
(U.S. Geological Survey published record)

[Concentrations in milligrams per liter; Max, maximum value; Min, minimum value; --, missing data]

DAY	APR	MAY	JUNE	JULY	AUG	SEPT	OCT	NOV
1	10.7	8.3	6.1	3.9	6.5	5.7	6.5	9.0
2	10.5	8.3	5.6	3.9	6.1	5.8	6.7	8.9
3	10.2	8.1	5.5	4.0	5.6	5.6	6.9	8.9
4	10.0	8.4	5.5	4.2	5.2	5.4	6.9	8.9
5	10.0	8.4	5.9	4.4	5.1	5.3	7.0	9.0
6	10.2	8.3	5.7	4.4	5.1	5.4	7.3	9.2
7	10.2	8.1	5.8	4.7	4.9	5.2	7.9	9.2
8	10.2	8.1	6.0	4.6	5.0	4.9	7.8	9.1
9	10.2	8.2	6.2	4.9	4.9	5.0	7.7	9.0
10	10.3	7.9	6.4	5.0	4.8	5.4	7.9	9.0
11	10.4	7.6	6.4	5.1	4.8	5.9	7.9	9.0
12	10.4	7.4	6.3	5.0	4.6	6.0	7.6	9.0
13	10.3	7.4	6.4	4.6	4.5	6.0	7.7	9.4
14	10.0	7.5	6.3	--	5.0	6.0	7.5	9.8
15	9.9	7.6	5.9	--	5.8	6.0	7.6	9.9
16	9.7	7.3	5.3	4.6	6.0	5.9	7.5	9.8
17	9.4	7.0	4.6	4.4	5.9	5.8	7.5	9.5
18	9.2	6.7	4.2	4.2	5.8	5.7	7.8	9.4
19	9.1	6.3	4.2	--	5.7	6.6	8.0	9.1
20	9.1	5.9	4.5	--	5.5	--	8.2	8.9
21	9.2	5.8	4.7	--	5.4	--	8.4	8.7
22	9.2	5.5	4.8	--	5.4	7.6	8.6	8.8
23	9.2	5.3	4.7	--	5.6	7.7	8.8	8.8
24	9.0	5.4	4.6	--	5.6	7.6	8.9	8.5
25	8.8	6.0	4.5	4.3	5.8	7.5	9.0	8.5
26	8.4	6.1	4.1	4.5	5.8	7.4	9.0	9.2
27	8.0	6.1	4.0	4.6	5.9	7.2	9.1	9.0
28	8.2	6.2	3.9	5.1	6.0	7.0	9.1	--
29	8.4	6.8	3.6	5.5	6.0	6.9	9.0	--
30	8.4	7.1	3.7	--	6.0	6.6	8.9	--
31		6.8		6.4	5.7		8.9	
Mean	9.6	7.1	5.2	4.6	5.5	6.2	8.0	9.1
Max	10.7	8.4	6.4	6.4	6.5	7.7	9.1	9.9
Min	8.0	5.3	3.6	3.9	4.5	4.9	6.5	8.5

Table 21. Daily mean dissolved oxygen concentration, Delaware River at Chester, Pennsylvania (station number 01477050), April 1 to November 30, 2004.
(U.S. Geological Survey published record)

[Concentrations in milligrams per liter; Max, maximum value; Min, minimum value; --, missing data]

DAY	APR	MAY	JUNE	JULY	AUG	SEPT	OCT	NOV
1	11.4	7.7	5.0	5.1	4.3	5.3	6.7	7.0
2	11.3	7.6	5.0	4.9	4.2	5.2	6.7	7.0
3	11.1	7.5	4.9	4.8	4.0	5.1	6.8	7.1
4	10.9	7.3	4.8	4.9	3.9	4.9	6.9	7.2
5	11.0	7.3	5.1	5.2	3.8	5.0	7.3	7.6
6	10.9	7.1	5.4	5.1	3.9	5.7	7.5	7.8
7	10.7	7.0	5.3	5.1	4.1	5.7	7.6	7.8
8	10.6	7.2	5.3	5.1	4.3	5.3	--	7.7
9	10.5	7.4	5.3	5.0	4.5	5.8	--	7.7
10	10.5	7.4	5.2	4.9	4.6	5.4	--	7.7
11	10.5	7.2	5.4	4.8	4.9	5.0	--	7.9
12	10.5	--	5.5	--	4.8	4.8	--	7.9
13	10.8	7.8	5.7	4.8	5.0	4.7	--	8.3
14	10.5	7.8	5.9	4.3	4.8	4.8	--	8.4
15	10.4	7.8	5.9	4.4	--	5.2	--	8.4
16	10.2	7.6	5.4	4.5	--	5.1	--	8.4
17	9.9	7.2	4.9	4.4	5.0	4.9	--	8.3
18	9.4	6.9	4.7	4.4	5.2	5.4	--	8.2
19	8.8	6.4	4.6	4.3	5.3	6.2	7.0	8.1
20	8.5	5.9	4.8	4.1	5.3	7.0	7.1	8.1
21	8.4	5.6	5.1	3.9	5.4	7.2	7.1	8.0
22	8.3	5.1	5.4	3.9	5.4	7.3	7.0	8.0
23	8.3	5.1	5.1	3.9	5.4	7.3	7.0	7.9
24	8.3	5.3	5.0	3.9	5.5	7.3	--	7.9
25	8.3	5.7	4.8	4.3	5.7	7.1	--	8.1
26	8.1	5.6	4.6	4.6	5.7	6.9	--	8.5
27	7.8	5.6	4.8	4.8	5.5	6.8	6.7	8.6
28	7.8	5.3	5.0	4.7	5.3	6.6	6.7	9.0
29	7.9	5.0	5.1	4.5	5.3	--	6.7	9.4
30	7.9	4.9	5.1	4.1	5.3	--	6.8	9.4
31		4.9		3.9	5.4		6.8	
Mean	9.6	6.5	5.1	4.6	4.9	5.8	7.0	8.0
Max	11.4	7.8	5.9	5.2	5.7	7.3	7.6	9.4
Min	7.8	4.9	4.6	3.9	3.8	4.7	6.7	7.0

Appendix A

Temporary Pepacton Reservoir Spill Reduction Program
December 11, 2003

Given the unusually high storage level of Pepacton Reservoir and the total storage conditions in the New York City (NYC) Delaware Basin Reservoirs for this time of the year, the temporary program described below is being implemented to reduce the volume of water spilled from Pepacton Reservoir. The program will attempt to achieve a void, not to exceed five billion gallons, in Pepacton Reservoir through supplemental releases above normal conservation rates from the East Delaware Release Chamber and then maintain that void until January 31, 2004. This is a one-time temporary program implemented in response to extraordinary hydrologic conditions. The program is not part of any regular release program and does not establish a precedent for any future releases or actions.

Although the total volume of water spilled from Pepacton Reservoir will be reduced by this temporary program, it is unlikely that peak flows downstream will be significantly reduced. The spillway at Pepacton Reservoir provides substantial attenuation of peak flows downstream even when the reservoir is spilling. Pepacton Reservoir was not designed as a flood control reservoir; consequently, the Parties to the 1954 Supreme Court Decree strongly urge communities downstream of the reservoir to take all necessary and prudent actions to improve (1) awareness of flooding potential and (2) flood preparedness.

Temporary Pepacton Reservoir Spill Reduction Program:

1. Upon approval of this agreement by the Decree Parties, the City of New York will implement a temporary program to achieve limited reduction of Pepacton Reservoir storage through supplemental releases from the East Delaware Release Chamber.

2. The recommended rate of the supplemental release shall be established daily by NYC in consultation with the Delaware River Master. Releases above the normal conservation rate will be accounted for as "special releases" and be considered neither River Master directed nor conservation in accordance with DRBC Docket D-77-20 (Revision 6).

3. The River Master will manage the recommended supplemental releases in such a manner as to conserve the waters of the Delaware Basin in accordance with the following guidance -- The flood stage for the East Branch Delaware River at Fishs Eddy is 15.0 ft. Accordingly, supplemental releases will not be made when the river stage for the East Branch Delaware River at Fishs Eddy is above 13.0 ft. or is forecast to be above 13.0 ft. within 48 hours of a planned supplemental release from Pepacton Reservoir. This procedure may be modified at any time if additional information demonstrates that a lower cautionary stage should be used to limit the supplemental releases.

4. Supplemental releases may be suspended if ice conditions threaten flood prone areas of the East Branch.

5. Supplemental releases will be designed so that the combined discharge from the East Delaware Release Chamber and the Downsville Dam spillway does not exceed 2,000 cfs. All supplemental releases will be discontinued when the spillway discharge exceeds 2,000 cfs.

6. When the storage level in Pepacton Reservoir is 5 billion gallons below full capacity, supplemental releases will be made as necessary to maintain that level to the extent possible throughout December 2003 and January 2004.

7. This program may be extended beyond January 2004, on a monthly basis, upon unanimous consent of the Decree Parties, depending upon total storage conditions in the New York City Delaware Basin Reservoirs and snow pack conditions in the watersheds upstream of those reservoirs.

8. This program may be terminated at any time at the request of any Decree Party, or may be modified with the unanimous consent of the Decree Parties.

Consent to Action by

The City of New York

Consent of the Parties to the U.S. Supreme Court Decree in New Jersey v. New York, 347 U.S. 995 (1954) approving the Temporary Pepacton Reservoir Spill Reduction Program by the City of New York.

/s/ Ernest P. Hahn		/s/ Fred Nuffer	
State of New Jersey	Date	State of New York	Date

/s/ Kevin C. Donnelly		/s/ Cathy Curran Myers	
State of Delaware	Date	Commonwealth of Pennsylvania	Date

/s/ John H. Talley		/s/ Michael A. Principe	
State of Delaware	Date	City of New York	Date

Appendix B

Temporary Pepacton Reservoir Spill Reduction Program
December 11, 2003
Revision 1. -- February 5, 2004

Given the unusually high storage level of Pepacton Reservoir and the total storage conditions in the New York City (NYC) Delaware Basin Reservoirs for this time of the year, the temporary program described below is being implemented to reduce the volume of water spilled from Pepacton Reservoir. The program will attempt to manage a void in Pepacton Reservoir, based on snowpack in the reservoir's watershed, through supplemental releases above normal conservation rates from the East Delaware Release Chamber and maintain that void until March 15, 2004. This is a one-time temporary program implemented in response to extraordinary hydrologic conditions. The program is not part of any regular release program and does not establish a precedent for any future releases or actions.

Although the total volume of water spilled from Pepacton Reservoir will be reduced by this temporary program, it is unlikely that peak flows downstream will be significantly reduced. The spillway at Pepacton Reservoir provides substantial attenuation of peak flows downstream even when the reservoir is spilling. Pepacton Reservoir was not designed as a flood control reservoir; consequently, the Parties to the 1954 Supreme Court Decree strongly urge communities downstream of the reservoir to take all necessary and prudent actions to improve (1) awareness of flooding potential and (2) flood preparedness.

Temporary Pepacton Reservoir Spill Reduction Program:

1. Upon approval of this agreement by the Decree Parties, the City of New York will implement a temporary program to achieve limited reduction of Pepacton Reservoir storage through supplemental releases from the East Delaware Release Chamber.

2. The recommended rate of the supplemental release shall be established daily by NYC in consultation with the Delaware River Master. Releases above the normal conservation rate will be accounted for as "special releases" and be considered neither River Master directed nor conservation in accordance with DRBC Docket D-77-20 (Revision 6).

3. The River Master will manage the recommended supplemental releases in such a manner as to conserve the waters of the Delaware Basin in accordance with the following guidance -- The flood stage for the East Branch Delaware River at Fishs Eddy is 15.0 ft. Accordingly, supplemental releases will not be made when the river stage for the East Branch Delaware River at Fishs Eddy is above 13.0 ft. or is forecast to be above 13.0 ft. within 48 hours of a planned supplemental release from Pepacton Reservoir. This procedure may be modified at any time if additional information demonstrates that a lower cautionary stage should be used to limit the supplemental releases.

4. Supplemental releases may be suspended if ice conditions threaten flood prone areas of the East Branch.

5. Supplemental releases will be designed so that the combined discharge from the East Delaware Release Chamber and the Downsville Dam spillway does not exceed 2,000 cubic feet per second (cfs). All supplemental releases will be discontinued when the spillway discharge exceeds 2,000 cfs.

6. When the storage elevation in Pepacton Reservoir is at or above the elevation equivalent to 5 billion gallons below full capacity, supplemental releases will be made as necessary to maintain that level to the extent possible throughout the term of this program. The 5 billion gallon void will be maintained only when 50 percent of water equivalent of snowpack in the Pepacton Reservoir watershed is greater than or equal to 5 billion gallons. If 50 percent of the snowpack water equivalent falls to a level below 5 billion gallons, supplemental releases will be discontinued.

7. This program will expire on March 15, 2004. The program may be terminated at any time at the request of any Decree Party or may be modified with the unanimous consent of the Decree Parties.

Consent to Action by

The City of New York

Consent of the Parties to the U.S. Supreme Court Decree in New Jersey v. New York, 347 U.S. 995 (1954), approving Revision 1 of the Temporary Pepacton Reservoir Spill Reduction Program by the City of New York.

/s/ Ernest P. Hahn	/s/ Fred Nuffer
State of New Jersey Date	State of New York Date
/s/ Kevin C. Donnelly	/s/ Cathy Curran Myers
State of Delaware Date	Commonwealth of Pennsylvania Date
/s/ John H. Talley	/s/ Michael A. Principe
State of Delaware Date	City of New York Date

Appendix C

NO. 2004-3
DOCKET NO. D-77-20 CP (Revision 7)
DELAWARE RIVER BASIN COMMISSION

A RESOLUTION, superseding and incorporating as necessary certain provisions of Resolutions D-77-20 CP Revision 2) through D-77-20 CP (Revision 6), to establish an experimental augmented conservation release program for the New York City Delaware Basin Reservoirs for the period beginning May 1, 2004 and ending May 31, 2007, and to engage in discussions to develop a longterm, flexible program to manage releases from the reservoirs.

WHEREAS, Docket No. D-77-20 CP (Revision 6) expires on April 30, 2004; and

WHEREAS, it is the objective of the Parties to the 1954 Supreme Court Decree, hereafter the Decree Parties, to develop a program for protecting tail water fisheries below New York City's Delaware Basin Reservoirs, hereafter City Delaware Reservoirs, based upon sustainable sources of water, while considering overall needs in the tailwaters below the City Delaware Reservoirs and in the main stem and bay; and

WHEREAS, the Delaware River Basin Commission (DRBC), through its Flow Management Technical Advisory Committee (FMTAC) and its Comprehensive Plan update process, is considering several approaches to assess overall needs in the tailwaters below the City Delaware Reservoirs and in the main stem and bay; and

WHEREAS, Docket No D-77-20 CP (Revision 6) provided that the New York City Department of Environmental Protection (NYCDEP) and the New York State Department of Environmental Conservation (NYSDEC) fund an update of the OASIS model and analysis of alternatives for an interim fisheries protection program for the City Delaware Reservoir tailwaters and, based on the results of this analysis, submit by September 30, 2003 a formal proposal for consideration by the Decree Parties and the DRBC for interim fisheries protection while discussions continue toward development of a long-term flexible reservoir releases program; and

WHEREAS, the State of New York has proposed an interim reservoir releases program to maintain target flows in the tailwaters below the City Delaware Reservoirs for the period beginning May 1, 2004, and ending May 31, 2007; and

WHEREAS, the proposed interim reservoir releases program will allow for more comprehensive and flexible management of releases in response to temperature and flow conditions in the New York City Delaware Basin reservoir tailwaters and upper main stem Delaware; and

WHEREAS, populations of dwarf wedgemussels, a federally- and state-listed endangered species, are known to exist in the Neversink River and mainstem Delaware River; and

WHEREAS, Resolution No. 2002-33 approved a "Drought Operations Plan for Lake Wallenpaupack", implementation of which is contingent upon the Decree Parties agreeing upon a reservoir releases program for the City Delaware Reservoirs that ameliorates any adverse impact of releases from Lake Wallenpaupack under the provisions of Resolution No. 2002-33; and

WHEREAS, NYSDEC, in collaboration with the Subcommittee on Ecological Flows (SEF) and the FMTAC, has developed a "Monitoring Plan for the Delaware River Tailwaters, 2004-2006" (Monitoring Plan), and

WHEREAS, the Monitoring Plan and the proposal described herein have been agreed to by all Decree Parties, now therefore,

BE IT RESOLVED by the undersigned Commissioners and Decree Parties:

1. The Decree Parties agree that development and implementation of a viable long-term program to address fisheries and other needs in the tailwaters below the City Delaware Reservoirs and in the main stem and bay requires consideration of other related issues, including interbasin transfer policy, Good Faith operations, New York City water supply needs, the DRBC Comprehensive Plan, the Basinwide Plan currently being developed, Montague flow targets, the Excess Release Quantity, and equitable apportionment of the waters of the Delaware Basin in accordance with the provisions of the 1954 Decree and the provisions of Docket D-77-20 CP as revised which are not being superseded hereby.

2. The Decree Parties commit to continuing discussions with the aid of the FMTAC guided by the Comprehensive Plan and the Basinwide Plan currently under development, with the objective of developing and implementing by May 31, 2007 a long-term, flexible program to manage releases from the City Delaware Reservoirs to better address fisheries in the tailwaters below the City Delaware Reservoirs. The long-term program must take into account needs in the main stem and the bay as well as the related issues recited in Paragraph 1 above.

3. During the effective period of the interim proposal, the following drought stage definitions and procedures will be in effect:

   A. Drought Watch.

   The seasonally segmented line (shown as dashes) splitting the current "Drought Warning" in Figure 1 of DRBC Resolution No. 83-13 and DRBC Docket No. D-77-20 CP (Revised) is temporarily raised by four (4) billion gallons during the entire year. In addition, the upper half of the drought warning, previously referred to as DWI, is temporarily renamed Drought Watch. Operations during the renamed Drought Watch shall continue to limit the diversion by New York City to 680 million gallons per day (mgd) and reduce the Montague and Trenton flow targets to 1,655 cubic feet per second (cfs) and 2,700 cfs, respectively. The New Jersey diversion will remain at 100 mgd.

   B. Drought Warning.

   The lower half of the drought warning (DW2), based upon the rule curves included in DRBC Resolution No. 83-13 and as temporarily modified by "A" above, is designated Drought Warning, with diversions and the flow targets at Montague and Trenton conforming to DRBC Resolution No. 83-13 for the former DW2.

   C. Drought Emergency.

   The Drought Emergency provision shall remain at the levels designated in DRBC Resolution No. 83-13.

   D. Balancing Adjustment.

   In order to conserve water, the Delaware River Master is requested to utilize a balancing adjustment when calculating the releases to be directed to meet the Montague target.

4. There is hereby established, for thermal and habitat protection in the tailwaters below the City Delaware Reservoirs, for the period beginning May 1, 2004 and ending May 31, 2007, a Habitat Protection Bank (HPB), with the following provisions:

   A. A "Habitat Protection Bank (HPB)" of 20,000 cubic feet per second days (cfs-days) is established, which shall consist of an Excess Release Quantity Bank (ERQB) of 5,700 cfs-days, provided from the Excess Release Quantity (ERQ); a Thermal Release Bank (TRB) of 9200 cfs-days; and a Supplemental Release Bank (SRB) of 5,100 cfs-days. Water from the ERQ shall be credited on June 15, and any water remaining from that quantity shall expire on March 15 of the following year. The 9,200 cfs-days TRB and 5,100 cfs-days SRB shall be credited on May 1, and any water remaining in these banks shall expire on April 30 of the following year. In any year during which the Drought Operations Plan for Lake Wallenpaupack is not in effect, the HPB shall be limited to 16,000 cfs-days, consisting of an ERQB of 3,420 cfs-days from the ERQ; a TRB of 9,200 cfs-days; and an SRB of 3,380 cfs-days. Waters from the ERQ not contributed to the HPB shall be utilized to provide a proportionally-reduced increase in the Montague flow objective according to the current procedures, or may be banked in accordance with the procedures outlined in the Lower Basin Drought Management Plan. In addition, an Amelioration Bank (AB) of 3,000 cfs-days may be available subject to the provisions of Paragraph 6.

B. The TRB shall be used to direct releases during May 1 through October 31 so as to prevent to the maximum extent possible any instantaneous water temperature higher than 75°F or any daily average temperature higher than 72°F in the designated downstream areas as determined from measurements at the Hale Eddy, Harvard, Bridgeville, Hancock and Hankins gaging stations. Designated downstream areas shall mean the following waters:

- The West Branch Delaware River between Cannonsville Reservoir and Hancock, NY

- The East Branch Delaware River between Pepacton Reservoir and the confluence of the East Branch Delaware and the Beaver Kill

- The Delaware River between Hancock, NY and Hankins, NY

- The Neversink River between Neversink Reservoir and Bridgeville, NY

Any quantity of water remaining in the TRB after October 31 may subsequently be used for habitat protection.

C. Upon entry into Drought Watch (Figure 1), the remaining quantity of water in the TRB and SRB shall be reduced by 15 percent. In addition, 2000 cfs-days of water from the Amelioration Bank (AB) would be made available subject to the provisions of Paragraph 6.

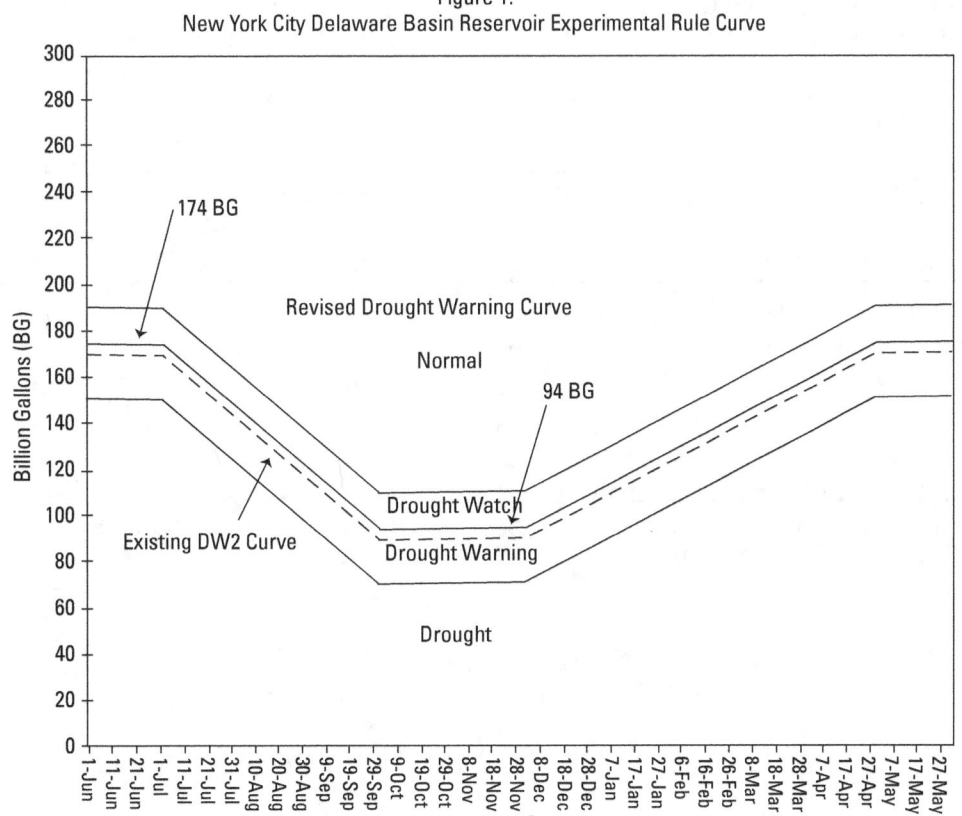

Figure 1.
New York City Delaware Basin Reservoir Experimental Rule Curve

D. Upon entry into Drought Warning (Figure 1), the remaining quantity of water in the TRB and SRB shall each be reduced by 15 percent. In addition, any water remaining of the available 2000 cfs-day AB would be made available subject to the provisions of Paragraph 6.

E. Upon entry into Drought (Figure 1), habitat and thermal protection may be provided, except as noted in Paragraph M, subject to the availability of the ERQB and at the discretion of the down-basin parties to the 1954 U.S. Supreme Court Decree. Any releases from the water remaining in the TRB and SRB shall be suspended until storage in the City Delaware Reservoirs is 25 billion gallons (BG) above the Drought Watch line for 15 consecutive days. The most severe set of conservation releases and tailwater flow targets realized as described in Paragraph F through M will remain in effect until storage in the City Delaware Reservoirs is 25 BG above the Drought Warning line for 15 consecutive days. In addition, any water remaining in the total AB would be made available subject to the provisions of Paragraph 6.

F. At the direction of the NYSDEC, the HPB may be used to meet the flow targets in Table 1.

Table 1
Habitat Protection Bank Flow Targets

| Target Location | -------------------- Flow Target (cfs) -------------------- | | | |
	Normal	Drought Watch	Drought Warning	Drought*
West Branch Delaware R At Hale Eddy	225	190	160	145
East Branch Delaware R at Harvard	175	150	120	115
Neversink River at Bridgeville	115	100	80	75

*Subject to the availability of the ERQB and the discretion of the down-basin parties to the 1954 U.S. Supreme Court Decree, or availability of the Amelioration Bank (AB).

G. Conservation releases from the City Delaware Reservoirs shall be as specified in Table 2 with additional releases directed by the NYSDEC to maintain tributary target flows as specified in Paragraph F.

Table 2
Conservation Releases

| Reservation | -------------- Conservation Release (cfs) -------------- | | | |
	Normal	Drought Watch	Drought Warning	Drought
Cannonsville (9/1–5/31)	45	38	32	23
Cannonsville (6/1–8/31)	60	51	43	23
Pepacton	35	30	25	19
Neversink	25	21	18	15

H. The difference between releases resulting from reservoir release operations specified in Paragraphs F and G, and the reference conservation releases specified in Table 3, shall be debited or credited to the HPB. However, a negative balance in the HPB is not allowed.

Table 3
Reference Conservation Releases

Reservoir and Operation Dates	Release Rate (cfs)			
	Normal	Drought Watch[1]	Drought Warning[2]	Drought[2]
Cannonsville				
1/1–4/15	45	38	8	8
4/16–5/31	45	38	23	23
6/1–9/15	160	136	23	23
9/16–11/30	45	38	23	23
12/1–12/31	45	38	8	8
Pepacton				
1/1–4/7	45	38	6	6
4/8–4/30	45	38	19	19
5/1–5/31	70	60	19	19
6/1–8/31	95	81	19	19
9/1–9/30	70	60	19	19
10/1–10/31	45	38	19	19
11/1–12/31	45	38	6	6
Neversink				
1/1–4/7	25	21	5	5
4/8–4/30	25	21	15	15
5/1–9/30	53	45	15	15
10/1–10/31	25	21	15	15
11/1–12/31	25	21	5	5

[1] 85 percent of the normal conservation release rates.

[2] Basic conservation release rates at specified in Table 4.

I. In the event that banks are exhausted, conservation releases continue as specified in Table 3.

J. No additional water beyond that specified in this resolution will be made available under any circumstances.

K. When the combined ERQB and SRB are exhausted, flow targets shall be suspended and only conservation releases as specified in Table 3 can be made, except after October 31 as provided in Paragraph 4 or at those times when the AB is available subject to the provisions of Paragraph 6.

L. In order to assure the delivery of high quality drinking water to New York City and neighboring outside communities, it may be necessary from time to time to decrease or cease the diversion of water from Cannonsville Reservoir, and increase the diversion of higher quality water from Neversink Reservoir. At such times, in order to conserve storage of Neversink Reservoir water, flow targeting at Bridgeville, N.Y. will be suspended and releases will be reduced to the augmented conservation release rates specified in Table 3. These program modifications will remain in effect until such time as Cannonsville Reservoir water quality improves to a level satisfying the criteria below. Prior to initiating such an action, the City of New York will consult with the Decree Parties. The suspension and re-initiation of flow targeting at Bridgeville will he based upon either of the following water quality criteria:

1) The diversion from Cannonsville Reservoir, based upon a 5-day running average, exceeds any of the following trigger levels for five key water quality parameters:

- Total Phosphorus = 20 μg/L
- Fecal coliform = 20 CFU/100 mL
- Total Coliform = 1000 CFU/100 mL
- Turbidity = 5 NTU
- Total Phytoplankton = 1000 SAU/mL; or

2) The water quality in the diversion from Cannonsville Reservoir, based upon a 5-day running average, exceeds 50% of any parameter indicated in Subparagraph (1) above and the difference in that value of the parameter is greater than 200% of the value of the same parameter in the diversion from Neversink Reservoir, based upon 5-day running averages.

(For example, if the turbidity exceeds 4 NTU in the diversion from Cannonsville Reservoir and is less than 2 NTU in the diversion from Neversink Reservoir, NYCDEP may temporarily suspend the flow target at Bridgeville and return to conservation releases as described in Table 3)

M. Should combined storage in Neversink, Pepacton, and Cannonsville Reservoirs drop below 25% usable capacity (i.e., less than 67.7 BG), water would be available for thermal mitigation by NYS-DEC, from the ERQB, subject to the discretion of the downbasin parties to the 1954 U.S. Supreme Court Decree, and flow targeting at Bridgeville, Harvard, and Hale Eddy will be suspended, until storage recovers to 5 billion gallons above the Drought Watch (Figure 1) tine for one day. Conservation releases will be made as specified in Table 4. Under this condition, there will be no debiting or crediting of the HPB, unless the ERQB has been made available, in which case there will be debiting of the ERQB.

5. NYSDEC shall conduct an evaluation in accordance with the Monitoring Plan. The evaluation shall assess the response of tailwater biota, particularly brown and rainbow trout populations, to the experimental release and target flow protocols established herein. The evaluation plan shall include the following components: evaluation need(s), purpose and scope, objectives, approach and methods, evaluation benefits, content of planned reports, evaluation schedule, personnel needs, budget, and source of funds. Where appropriate, results of previous investigations conducted as part of the historical experimental release program shall be included in the evaluation plan.

NYSDEC shall, on February 28, 2005 and February 28, 2006, submit to the DRBC and to the Decree Parties annual interim progress reports on the study. The initial report to be submitted on February 28,

Table 4
Basic Conservation Releases

Reservoir and Operation Dates	Release Rate (cfs)
Cannonsville	
4/1–4/15	8
4/16–11/30	23
12/1–3/31	8
Pepacton	
4/1–4/7	6
4/8–10/31	19
11/1–3/31	6
Neversink	
4/1–4/7	5
4/8–10/31	15
11/1–3/31	5

2005 shall incorporate summary data and conclusions obtained since the experimental release program was initiated in 1977. Discussion of such reports shall be included as an agenda item at annual meetings of the Delaware River Master Advisory Committee.

By December 31, 2006, NYSDEC shall submit a draft scientific report, which shall include an abstract or executive summary, statements of purpose, scope and objectives, procedures, results, conclusions, recommendations for additional work if warranted, and supporting literature, and shall describe effects on the fishery and other aquatic resources resulting from implementation of this resolution.

By May 31, 2007, NYSDEC shall submit a final scientific report.

6. In any year during which the Drought Operations Plan for Lake Wallenpaupack is in effect, if on May 1 the basin is not in Normal (see Figure 1), or if after May 1 the basin enters Drought Watch, an Amelioration Bank (AB) of 3,000 cfs-days will be created. During Drought Watch and Drought Warning (see Figure 1), a total of releases not to exceed 2,000 cfs-days may be made from the AB to meet the target flows according to Table 1. During Drought (see Figure 1), the remainder of the 3,000 cfs-day AB may be used to maintain conservation releases in accordance with Table 2 and for thermal protection in accordance with Paragraph 4.B. Any remaining AB will expire on April 30.

7. In any year during which the Drought Operations Plan for Lake Wallenpaupack is not in effect, releases for flow targeting will only he made from Cannonsville Reservoir for targets at Hale Eddy, to conserve the available bank. No releases will be made for flow targeting from Neversink or Pepacton Reservoirs. Releases from Neversink and Pepacton Reservoirs will be in accordance with Table 3.

8. The Commission and the Decree Parties will review and evaluate available data during the implementation of this program and will consider any modifications that may be necessary to avoid adverse effect to dwarf wedgemussels.

9. This resolution shall take effect upon consent by the Decree Parties and shall expire on May 31, 2007, or earlier either upon a determination by the down-basin parties to the 1954 Supreme Court Decree that the requirements of Paragraph 5 have not been met or when an alternative long-term tailwaters fisheries program, unanimously approved by the Decree Parties, is implemented.

10. Approval of and unanimous consent to this Resolution shall be deemed as approval of and consent to the reservoir releases program for the New York City Delaware River Basin reservoirs as specified in Article 3 of Resolution No. 2002-33.

11. For the effective period, this Resolution shall supersede Resolutions D-77-20 CP (Revision 2) through D-77-20 CP (Revision 6).

/s/ Fred Nuffer
Fred Nuffer, Acting Chairman pro tem

/s/ Pamela M. Bush
Pamela M. Bush, Esquire, Commission Secretary

ADOPTED: April 21, 2004

Consent to Action by

Delaware River Basin Commission

Consent of the Parties to the U.S. Supreme Court Decree in <u>New Jersey v. New York</u>, 347 U.S. 995 (1954) to the action of the Delaware River Basin Commission approving Resolution No. 2004-3, Docket No. D-77-20 CP (Revision 7), and amending the Comprehensive Plan with respect to experimental modifications to the schedule of release rates from Cannonsville, Pepacton and Neversink Reservoirs.

| /s/ Samuel A. Wolfe | 4/21/04 | /s/ Michael A. Principe | 4/21/04 |
| State of New Jersey | Date | City of New York | Date |

| /s/ John H. Talley | 4/21/04 | /s/ Fred Nuffer | 4/21/04 |
| State of Delaware | Date | State of New York | Date |

| /s/ Harry W. Otto | 4/21/04 | /s/ Cathy Curran Myers | 4/21/04 |
| State of Delaware | Date | Commonwealth of Pennsylvania | Date |

Appendix D

A RESOLUTION amending Docket No D-77-20 CP (Revision 7), to allow that portion of the Excess Release Quantity not earmarked for the program for protecting tailwater fisheries below New York City's Delaware Basin Reservoirs, to be used for purposes of aquatic resource research related to the fisheries program, including dwarf wedgemussel studies conducted at the request of the U.S. Fish and Wildlife Service.

WHEREAS, Docket No. D-77-20 CP (Revision 7) provides a program for protecting the tailwater fisheries below New York City's Delaware Basin Reservoirs for the period May 1, 2004 through May 31, 2007; and

WHEREAS, Docket No. D-77-20 CP (Revision 7) requires implementation of "Monitoring Plan for the Delaware River Tailwaters, 2004-2006"; and

WHEREAS, Docket No. D-77-20 CP (Revision 7) requires the Commission and the Decree Parties to review and evaluate available data during the implementation of the program and to consider any modifications that may be necessary to avoid adverse effect to dwarf wedgemussels; and

WHEREAS, regulation of flows in the tailwaters below New York City's Delaware Basin Reservoirs may facilitate implementation of certain aspects of the Monitoring Plan or collection of data related to the dwarf wedgemussels; now therefore,

BE IT RESOLVED by the Delaware River Basin Commission:

1. Paragraph 4.A of Docket No. D-77-20 CP (Revision 7) is hereby revised to read as follows (changes denoted by underscore):

   "A. 'Habitat Protection Bank (HPB)' of 20,000 cubic feet per second days (cfs-days) is established, which shall consist of: an Excess Release Quantity Bank (ERQB) of 5,700 cfs-days, provided from the Excess Release Quantity (ERQ), a Thermal Release Bank (TRB) of 9,200 cfs-days, and a Supplemental Release Bank (SRB) of 5,100 cfs-days. Water from the ERQ shall be credited on June 15, and any water remaining from that quantity shall expire on March 15 of the following year. The 9,200 cfs-days TRB and 5,100 cfs-days SRB shall he credited on May 1, and any water remaining in these banks shall expire on April 30 of the following year. In any year during which the Drought Operations Plan for Lake Wallenpaupack is not in effect, the HPB shall he limited to 16,000 cfs-days, consisting of: an ERQB of 3,420 cfs-days from the ERQ; a TRB of 9,200 cfs-days; and an SRB of 3,380 cfs-days. Waters from the ERQ not contributed to the HPB shall be utilized for any of the following purposes or any combination thereof: (1) to provide a proportionally-reduced increase in the Montague flow objective according to the current procedures, (2) to be banked in accordance with the procedures outlined in the Lower Basin Drought Management Plan, or (3) for the purpose of facilitating aquatic resources research related to the program for protecting tailwater fisheries below the City Delaware Reservoirs, including related dwarf wedgemussel studies conducted at the request of the U.S. Fish and Wildlife Service. In the latter case, Decree Party approval is required for each aquatic resources research project undertaken. In addition, an Amelioration Bank (AB) of 3,000 cfs-days may be available subject to the provisions of Paragraph 6."

2. In all other respects, Docket No. D-77-20 CP (Revision 7) shall remain in full force and effect.

3. The Decree Parties agree to inform the Commission and the Subcommittee on Ecological Flows promptly when they approve a research project under the above provision.

/s/ Fred Nuffer
Fred Nuffer, Chairman *pro tem*

/s/ Pamela M. Bush
Pamela M. Bush, Esq., Commission Secretary

ADOPTED: July 13, 2004

Consent to Action by

Delaware River Basin Commission

Consent of the parties to the U.S. Supreme Court Decree in *New Jersey v. New York*, 347 U.S. 995 (1954) to the action of the Delaware River Basin Commission approving Resolution No. 2004-9, Docket No. D-77-20 CP (Revision 8) and amending the Comprehensive Plan with respect to uses of the portion of the Excess Release Quantity not dedicated to the fisheries program approved by Resolution No. 2004-3.

/s/ Ernest P. Hahn	9/1/04	/s/ Michael A. Principe	9/9/04
State of New Jersey	Date	City of New York	Date

/s/ Harry W. Otto	7/13/04	/s/ Fred Nuffer	8/3/04
State of Delaware	Date	State of New York	Date

/s/ John H. Talley	8/6/04	/s/ Cathy Curran Myers	8/1/04
State of Delaware	Date	Commonwealth of Pennsylvania	Date

Appendix E

Temporary Bottom Release Program for Cannonsville and Pepacton Reservoirs

**Prepared August 17, 2004 by the New York State Department of
Environmental Conservation and the
New York City Department of Environmental Protection**

In response to abnormally high storage levels of Pepacton and Cannonsville Reservoirs, the persistent wet weather, and continuing high runoff, a temporary bottom release program will be implemented to reduce the quantity of warm surface water that will spill from the reservoirs. The warm water may have adverse impacts on cold-water species in the East and West Branches of the Delaware River.

In order to reduce the amount of warm water spillage, the following program of cold water bottom releases will be implemented:

1. Bottom releases will be considered when the void in Pepacton Reservoir or Cannonsville Reservoir is less than 3 BG.

2. Upon reaching the 3 BG threshold, the bottom release quantity for the day will be computed in the following manner using data from the 8:00 a.m. NYCDEP Water Supply Report:

   a. Case 1: Void less than 3 BG and greater than 0.5 BG:

      i. Available Program Release Volume = Runoff minus diversion minus 200 MG or the normal conservation release, whichever is greater (Goal is to allow reservoir storage to increase at the rate of 200 MGD).

      ii. *Actual release rates will be determined by NYSDEC based on the available program release volume.*

   b. Case 2: Void less than 0.5 BG:

      i. Available Program Release Volume = Runoff minus diversion or the normal conservation release, whichever is greater.

      ii. *Actual release rates will be determined by NYSDEC based on the available program release volume.*

3. Release rates will be stepped up and stepped down in accordance with the standard DEC protocol of no more than 100 cfs per hour.

4. Releases will not be charged to existing thermal or habitat banks.

5. Program will terminate on September 30, 2004.

Consent to Action by The City of New York

Consent of the Parties to the U.S. Supreme Court Decree in New Jersey v. New York, 347 U.S. 995 (1954), approving the Temporary Pepacton and Cannonsville Reservoir Bottom Release Program by the City of New York.

/s/ Ernest P. Hahn		/s/ Fred Nuffer	
State of New Jersey	Date	State of New York	Date

/s/ Kevin C. Donnelly		/s/ Cathy Curran Myers	
State of Delaware	Date	Commonwealth of Pennsylvania	Date

/s/ John H. Talley		/s/ Kurt Rieke	
State of Delaware	Date	City of New York	Date

USGS

Printed on recycled paper